for the
Love
of the
Land

A cook book to celebrate British Farmers and their food

Compiled by Jenny Jefferies

For the Love of the Land

©2020 Jenny Jefferies & Meze Publishing Ltd. All rights reserved

First edition printed in 2020 in the UK

ISBN: 978-1910863-58-9

Compiled by: Jenny Jefferies

Edited by: Katie Fisher

Photography by: Paul Greogry, Matt Crowder & Simon Burt

Additional photography: Thomas Alexander Photography, TH Photography, www.geoffreardon.com, ettores/shutterstock.com, National Farmers Union

Designed by: Paul Cocker

Contributors: Michael Johnson, Sarah Koriba, Paul Stimpson

Printed in Great Britain by Bell and Bain Ltd, Glasgow

Published by Meze Publishing Limited
Unit 1b, 2 Kelham Square
Kelham Riverside
Sheffield S3 8SD
Web: www.mezepublishing.co.uk
Telephone: 0114 275 7709
Email: info@mezepublishing.co.uk

FOREWORD

BY MINETTE BATTERS, PRESIDENT OF THE NATIONAL FARMERS' UNION

If there's one thing we do well in the UK, it's producing delicious, wholesome, nutritious food to fill our plates: food that's renowned around the world for its incredible flavours, affordability and high production standards.

We have a thriving food culture in this country and a passion for creating something extraordinary out of humble home-grown ingredients. Much of this has originated from a closer link between farmers, chefs and the public, and a sense of pride in what we are creating. It's great to see more and more chefs championing local ingredients and really showcasing the quality food we're producing on home soil.

But this all means nothing without a prosperous farming sector. And you know what they say; behind every great British ingredient is a great British farmer.

The backbone of rural communities, farming is at the core of our cultural heritage. Farmers are the central cog of the great machine that is our food and drink industry, which contributes more than £120 billion to the national bank and provides jobs for around four million people. Come wind or rain, our farmers are the people we rely on to keep us fed day in, day out.

It's exciting to see shoppers wanting to know more about the people behind their food, and in the UK we have a truly fantastic story to tell. For our farmers, producing quality food goes hand in hand with caring for the environment. We are the original custodians of the countryside and for generations we've shaped the iconic landscapes we know and love today. We are also leading the way in climate-friendly food production.

Whether it's our environmental credentials, sustainable food systems or high animal welfare standards, we can say with pride that our food truly embodies the values our nation holds dear.

Every single person can play their part in championing UK food and farming by looking out for the Union Jack Red Tractor logo when shopping. And when you're whipping up these delicious recipes, remember that you too are part of the story of great British food.

CONTENTS

ABOUT THIS BOOK

"The aim of this book is to bridge the gap between city and country, food and technology; to educate and inform; to connect and entertain; and to share the dedication of those who produce our food, in the words of the farmers themselves. This is not only a cook book, but a slice of British social history that will take you on a compelling journey through our beautiful Isles with evocative images, words, and of course food. Their love of the land is inspiring and should be shared and celebrated." – Jenny Jefferies

We have brought together a wide range of voices from the British farming industry in this book, celebrating their invaluable contributions to the food that ends up on our table. Some grow arable crops, some raise livestock, others specialise in fields of lavender or acres of garlic. They all play a hugely important part in the story of British farming, despite the many obstacles and hardships faced in these toughest of jobs.

From two young women who lost their father and took on the family farm in Shetland, to a portable urban farm in Hull that strives to educate city-dwellers about provenance, the people and places within these chapters have told their stories with honesty and passion. Commitment to sustainable practices, protecting the environment and preserving Britain's farming traditions alongside using technology to achieve progress are just some of the common themes in their descriptions of their livelihoods. Being hungry farmers, they have also got plenty of recipes under their belts, many of which have been shared in these pages, from Blackbrook Beef Bolognese to Kentish Lavender Shortbread.

For many of us, 2020 has brought more time than ever to spend at home, perhaps reconnecting with cooking when our food options were limited and thinking about how to support our local businesses, neighbours, families and friends throughout the most difficult months the country has endured for decades. In this light, having fresh homegrown produce available looks even more crucial to our health and wellbeing, so let's recognise the people who never stopped working hard to keep shelves stocked and plates full.

Find out more about the British farmers and producers near you in the Directory at the back of this book: pay your local farm shop a visit, get an insight to farming life on social media or spend a day amongst the fields at PYOs and open farm weekends. We hope that this book inspires you to reconnect with the food that you buy and eat, encouraging a new understanding of what it takes for our farmers to produce it and the ways they are preserving not just a way of life, but the very land that provides it.

DEDICATION

BY JENNY JEFFERIES

For John, Heidi & Florence.

After marrying my husband, John, I discovered the wonderful, challenging and sometimes isolating world of farming. I had never before quite appreciated where our food came from. It's been a real privilege to speak with the farmers within this book; they are truly the backbone of our country. They nurture and provide for us, putting food on our table for us to enjoy. Let's give thanks and praise for all the hard work that they do. This book has become a labour of love and I hope this collection of stories and of the farmers' favourite recipes is simply enjoyed for its food, provenance and for the sharing of positive stories. This is a celebration of British farming. Enjoy!

A proportion of the royalties from each copy of this book will be donated to The National Literacy Trust, a charity dedicated to giving disadvantaged children the literacy skills they need to succeed. More information on the NLT can be found at www.literacytrust.org.uk

Free resources of information about farming for use by teachers can be found at www.leafuk.org/education/leaf-education and www.countrysideclassroom.org.uk

THE BEAR AND BLACKSMITH

BY CLAIRE TALL

"I think that the farming way of life is idyllic but also hard work, and producing one's own food is more satisfying than anything else."

The Bear and Blacksmith is a small pub situated in the heart of Chillington, a village in the South Hams, South Devon. My partner, Malcolm, and I are the landlord and landlady and Malcolm is also chef patron. Alongside the pub, we both run a 70+ acre farm where we rear sheep, pigs and poultry which supplies the pub all year round. We also grow a lot of the vegetables, fruits and herbs in a kitchen garden, next to the beer garden, where customers can watch the chefs picking produce for the kitchen.

I was brought up on a dairy and sheep farm, and I do believe that farming is in my blood. I think that the farming way of life is idyllic but also hard work, and producing one's own food is more satisfying than anything else. From their birth, we help to rear and nurture our lambs on the most natural feeds and lush meadow grasses, and when the time comes for them to go to slaughter, we are then able to process the carcasses at our own butchery situated on the farm, and can decide which cuts we need for new and exciting dishes on the pub's menu.

The customers are in awe of our 'farm to fork' ethos and the quality of our produce; the fantastic food we serve has won us many awards and accolades in our two years thus far of running The Bear and Blacksmith. I believe that there has been a turning point in the public's interest in food production, animal welfare and food mileage, and here at our pub we can boast that we are 'ultra local' by using the finest ingredients and beverages that are literally on our doorstep. Why would we use anything that has travelled miles when we have the best and richest harvest here in Devon? We are five minutes from the sea and we only buy fish and shellfish from the day boat fishermen from Salcombe or Brixham, and if the wind is blowing and the fishermen can't get to the crab pots, then crab simply comes off the menu.

The future for The Bear and Blacksmith is to carry on expanding the farm to enable us to rear South Devon beef cattle, to offer education to the local youth, to offer butchery and cooking demonstrations and to promote the best of what our local area has to offer.

HERB CRUSTED RACK OF LAMB WITH BUTTERNUT SQUASH SAAG ALOO AND PARSNIP CRISPS

At The Bear and Blacksmith we often like to experiment with the meat we have available and accompanying vegetables and herbs we have grown in our polytunnel, kitchen garden or from surrounding farms to highlight seasonality. The menu is dictated by the farm and garden, not the other way round. – Claire Tall

4 French-trimmed racks of lamb (each with 3 bones)

Olive or rapeseed oil

Salt and pepper

For the herb crust

200g breadcrumbs

Handful of parsley, roughly chopped

Handful of coriander, roughly chopped

2 cloves of garlic, finely chopped

1 tsp mild curry powder

½ tsp ground cumin

For the butternut squash saag aloo

1 butternut squash, peeled and diced into 2.5cm cubes

Pinch of cayenne pepper

½ tsp ground cumin

½ tsp turmeric

Few sprigs of thyme

2 cloves of garlic, finely chopped

500g spinach leaves

For the parsnip crisps

1 parsnip

Vegetable oil

For the coriander oil

Large handful of coriander leaves

Good quality extra-virgin olive oil

Brush the racks of lamb with oil and season each one. Sear them in a hot pan until the meat is golden and sealed all over, then transfer them into a roasting tin. Combine all the ingredients for the herb crust in a bowl until well mixed, then pack some on top of each rack of lamb.

Roast the racks of lamb in the oven at 150°c until the meat reaches 45°c when probed. This should take about 35 to 40 minutes.

At the same time, mix the butternut squash with the spices, thyme and garlic then add a good glug of oil and spread out in a roasting tin. Roast the squash at 150°c for approximately 30 minutes until tender but not losing its shape. When done, remove the tin from the oven and stir in the spinach leaves so they wilt.

Leave the racks of lamb to rest while you make the garnishes. Peel the parsnip then shave off long strips with a potato peeler. Deep fry the parsnip shavings in a deep fat fryer, or a large pan half filled with vegetable oil, until they are crisp. Place them on kitchen paper to drain and season with salt. Finally, blitz the coriander with the extra-virgin olive oil in a blender or food processor, then season to taste.

To serve

Spoon some saag aloo onto a hot plate, place the rack of lamb on top, decorate with parsnip crisps and drizzle coriander oil around the dish.

PREPARATION TIME: 20-25 MINUTES | COOKING TIME: 45-50 MINUTES | SERVES: 4

BEESWAX DYSON FARMING

BY LAURA SMITHSON

"Our methods and innovative practices work in harmony with nature to enhance biodiversity, improve soil fertility and conserve the environment while growing highly nutritious food without diminishing our natural capital."

Beeswax Dyson Farming is a family-owned agricultural company growing a diverse range of quality products. Farming is at the heart of what we do; we proudly farm and manage the land in a sustainable way across Lincolnshire, Oxfordshire and Gloucestershire.

We grow a diverse range of food products, with varied rotations that enable us to produce crops for both food and renewable energy. Our cattle and sheep help us to better utilise and manage permanent pastures and parkland. More recently, in 2019 we began selling our beef direct to customers through a farm shop in Gloucestershire. We work hard to shorten the supply chain between consumers and farmers so that they can understand more about how we farm and we can adjust our systems to produce the food they want.

Technology and innovation play a large part in our farming methods. Our two anaerobic digestion plants in Lincolnshire produce enough electricity to power 10,000 homes. We work closely with machinery manufacturers, research institutes and technology companies to improve the efficiency and safety of farm machinery while implementing practices to safeguard soil health.

Beeswax Dyson Farming is a very special company to work for. It truly feels like a family, and our commitment to a long-term plan, that leaves a positive land legacy in 100 years' time, is inspiring. I have worked in the Property and Estate team since 2015, managing the Lincolnshire residential and commercial portfolio. Coming from a farming background, I have always had a keen interest in country life... A true passion of mine is cooking using seasonal and locally sourced produce, experimenting in the kitchen to come up with exciting dishes.

PEA AND MINT CROQUETTES
WITH A BEETROOT YOGHURT DIP

· ·

This recipe reflects the seasonal produce from Beeswax Dyson Farming. The classic and familiar potato croquette has been given a modern edge with flavours of pea and fresh mint. This dish can either be served as a starter or alongside roast lamb.
– Laura Smithson

For the croquettes

400g floury potatoes (such as King Edwards or Mozart)

150g peas

1 tsp butter

40g Gruyère cheese, grated

1 medium egg yolk

Small bunch of mint, finely chopped

30g plain flour

2 medium eggs, beaten

60g panko breadcrumbs

For the dip

4 medium beetroots

Rapeseed oil

1 lemon, zested and juiced

Small bunch of mint, chopped

6 tbsp plain yoghurt

For the croquettes

Preheat the oven to 200°c. Peel and chop the potatoes, place them in a pan of lightly salted boiling water and cook for 15 minutes, or until tender. Meanwhile, cook the peas for 5 minutes in a pan of lightly salted boiling water then drain.

Drain the potatoes and put them back into the pan over a low heat to steam off any excess water for 1 minute. Mash the potatoes with the butter then beat in the cheese and egg yolk until fully combined. Lightly crush the peas and stir these into the potatoes along with the chopped mint.

Leave the mixture to cool until it's the right temperature to handle. Divide into 12 balls. Put the flour, eggs and panko breadcrumbs into three separate bowls. Dip each croquette into the flour, knocking off any excess, then into the egg mix and finally into the panko breadcrumbs, covering each ball well. Drizzle with rapeseed oil and bake in the preheated oven for 30 minutes or until golden.

For the dip

This can be made ahead and kept in the fridge. Wash and trim the beets, leaving the skin and roots on. Lightly oil and place them in an ovenproof dish then cover with tin foil and place in the preheated oven for 1 hour 30 minutes or until tender and easily pierced with a knife.

Once cooked, peel off and discard the skins, roughly chop the beets and place in a blender. Season with salt and pepper, add a glug of rapeseed oil, the lemon zest, half the lemon juice and all the chopped mint. Blitz until smooth. Stir in the yoghurt and check the seasoning, adding more lemon juice, salt and pepper if required. Serve the dip with the warm croquettes.

PREPARATION TIME: 30 MINUTES | COOKING TIME: I HOUR 30 MINUTES | SERVES: I2

BIGTON FARM

BY AIMEE BUDGE

"My sister and I are young female farmers, which is quite unusual, but we are passionate about farming and believe we can do as good a job as anybody. We are enthusiastic about sharing our story and encouraging young people to get into farming."

I am passionate about rearing good quality meat to high welfare standards. I love working with the land to produce feed for our livestock, ensuring our meat is reared in harmony with nature. We have 90 suckler cattle which are kept outside all year round, only taking them inside for calving. This keeps them fit and healthy, and means we can save on straw for bedding. We also have 500 Shetland Cheviot cross breeding ewes and 100 pure Shetland ewes, allowing us to breed our own replacements. In addition, we grow 60 acres of spring barley to produce feed for our livestock and sell the surplus to our farming neighbours.

I run the business alongside my sister, Kirsty, and our mum plays a huge role by supporting us in our decision-making and helping us nearly every day along with our grandad and Uncle Jim; we couldn't do this without them. My sister and I took over the family business in 2014 when our dad died in a tragic farming accident. This has been very hard to deal with but we have got through it with the strong support from our family. We are the fifth generation to farm the land at Bigton and this means a lot to us: we are proud to carry on this long family tradition.

My sister and I are young female farmers, which is quite unusual, but we are passionate about farming and believe we can do as good a job as anybody. We are enthusiastic about sharing our story to demonstrate what is possible with resilience and strength, and hope to encourage young people to get into farming by offering work experience placements and using social media. We recently hosted Open Farm Sunday to show the public where their food comes from; this was a huge success and around 200 people visited the farm.

It's especially important to target the next generation, so we have had school visits on our farm to teach children where their food comes from as well. We featured on BBC's This Farming Life and had a great response from everyone, especially our community. I won BFAs Agriculture Student of the Year in 2018 which was an amazing honour, and in the same year Kirsty and I won Countryfile Farming Heroes. We want to encourage everyone to buy local and enjoy high quality meat and dairy produce, so we can all protect the environment by supporting British farmers.

REESTIT MUTTON SOUP

Reestit mutton is a traditional recipe from Shetland. Mutton leg or shoulder is left in a salt pickle for about two weeks, then dried for about a month, traditionally on a pulley in the kitchen. This soup is a great winter warmer, after a morning on the croft in gale force winds and lashing rain. – Aimee Budge

500g reestit mutton

6 tatties (potatoes)

1 small turnip

4 carrots

1 leek

Boil the reestit mutton for 1 hour in a large pot, pouring off the water and adding freshly boiled water throughout the cooking time.

While this boils, peel and cut up the potatoes, turnip, carrots and leek. After the first hour, add all the vegetables to the pot with the mutton and boil for another hour, stirring occasionally to stop it sticking to the bottom of pot. Add extra boiled water if the liquid gets too thick.

Take the reestit mutton out of the pot and transfer it onto a plate. Cut the meat into chunks, ladle the soup into bowls and then serve with a generous helping of reestit mutton on top of each portion.

PREPARATION TIME: 30 MINUTES | COOKING TIME: 2 HOURS | SERVES: 6

THE BLACK FARMER

BY WILFRED EMMANUEL-JONES

"I was completely taken aback by the huge sense of community here, something I hadn't experienced since my very early childhood in Jamaica...I was and continue to be really grateful for the support and advice I received from my farming neighbours."

When I first bought my farm near Launceston on the Devon-Cornwall border, it was the fulfilment of a dream I had spent 40 years of my life working to achieve: a very small piece of real farming country where livestock produces fantastic meat and dairy thanks to the quality of farming and lush meadows for grazing.

But above and beyond that, the real charm of this location is that it belongs to a time gone by. As an urbanite, I was completely taken aback by the huge sense of community here, something I hadn't experienced since my very early childhood in Jamaica. In our towns and cities, we are spoilt with the variety of public services on offer. In these rural communities, if you have a problem you have only each other to rely on.

When I first appeared in the area, I was and continue to be really grateful for the support and advice I received from my farming neighbours. In fact, I was the first black person many of my neighbours had met and it is due to them that my brand name – The Black Farmer – came about, as that is how I was known locally.

The following recipe for Shepherd's Pie is one of my favourites, and uses lamb in the true tradition of this dish. It takes me back to the early days when I had just bought my farm and I decided to buy a small flock of lambs. I had never bought animals before, and I was hugely excited. I went with my family and friends to the livestock market at Hallworthy on New Year's Day and, with lots of advice and guidance from the local farming community, I bought myself 20 sheep. It was then that the reality of keeping animals dawned on me. Sheep seem to have an innate desire to escape or get up to other antics!

Mine was a fairly short-lived love affair with keeping these animals, but it gave me even more respect for my farming neighbours who produce our meat and tend the land. Day in, day out, whatever the weather, animal husbandry and caring for the land – be it milking, hedging, ploughing – has no respite. It's hard graft that follows generations of tradition. For me, making sure that The Black Farmer brand put British farming on the map became my priority, and I leave the rest of it to those who know how!

SHEPHERD'S PIE

· ·

For a twist on a regular shepherd's pie and as a nod to my Jamaican birthplace, I've mashed sweet potatoes with white ones. Not only does this add a sweetness that goes so well with the lamb, the golden topping looks wonderfully appetising. Serve with a simple green salad to cut through the delicious richness. – Wilfred Emmanuel-Jones

I tbsp olive oil

I large onion, finely chopped

2 carrots, finely diced

2 sticks of celery, finely diced

2 cloves of garlic, crushed

500g lean lamb mince

75ml dark Jamaican rum

2 tbsp Worcestershire sauce

400g tinned chopped tomatoes

I vegetable stock cube

I tbsp dried mixed herbs

Salt and freshly ground black pepper

50g hard Devonshire goat's cheese, grated

For the potato mash topping

750g floury potatoes, cut into chunks

500g sweet potatoes, cut into chunks

2 tbsp milk

25g butter

Heat the oil in a wide, deep pan with a lid and gently cook the onion, carrots, celery and garlic for 8 to 10 minutes until soft and translucent, but not brown. Add the lamb mince, breaking it up with a wooden spoon, and cook for 5 minutes until brown.

Add the rum and bubble for a few minutes until nearly evaporated. Stir in the Worcestershire sauce, chopped tomatoes, vegetable stock cube and mixed herbs. Season with salt and black pepper and turn the heat down low. Cover tightly with a lid and simmer for I hour.

For the potato mash topping

Meanwhile, put the potatoes and sweet potatoes in a large pan of salted water and bring to the boil. Simmer for 20 minutes until tender. Drain thoroughly, return to the pan and mash until smooth. Then stir in the milk and butter until combined. Season generously and set aside.

Preheat the oven to 190°c. Spoon the meat mixture into a 1.5 litre ovenproof dish and cover with the mashed potato. If you are feeling fancy, you can pipe the mash on top. Sprinkle with the grated goat's cheese.

Cook in the oven for 30 minutes until golden and bubbling. Serve immediately. To make the shepherd's pie ahead, cover the assembled pie and then chill in the fridge for up to 2 days, or freeze. Bring the pie back to room temperature or defrost thoroughly before cooking as above.

PREPARATION TIME: 15 MINUTES | COOKING TIME: APPROX. 1 HOUR | SERVES: 4-6

THE BLACK SWAN

BY THE BANKS

"Naturally, we wanted to grow our own produce, so in 2013 a three acre kitchen garden was developed in the field next to the restaurant. Having the garden allowed us to grow food that was unique to us, such as crapaudine beetroot, black truffle potatoes and wineberries."

The Banks family have lived and farmed around Oldstead for many generations; it is very much our creation and passion. We opened The Black Swan Oldstead on 1st August 2006 (Yorkshire Day!) and Tommy's recent venture, Roots York, opened on 15th September 2018 in partnership with Matthew Lockwood. Tommy Banks is chef owner of both restaurants.

Naturally, we wanted to grow our own produce, so in 2013 a three acre kitchen garden was developed in the field next to the restaurant. Having the garden allowed us to grow food that was unique to us, such as crapaudine beetroot, black truffle potatoes and wineberries. This led to the family farm being used for growing as well. Many of the annual vegetables such as beetroot, peas, beans, carrots, potatoes, chicories, brassica and squash are now being produced on the farm in larger quantities to keep up with demand from the two restaurants.

Some crops such as sweetcorn and lettuces require a little more attention, or benefit from food metres rather than food miles, and where this is the case, these are cultivated in the garden amongst the perennial herbs. Some of these are even harvested while the guests are dining just before they are cooked, which really does showcase the freshness of the produce and our 'garden to table' ethos.

Produce is also preserved throughout the harvest months to ensure Oldstead produce can be used year round. Instead of the traditional four seasons, we work with three key seasons that link to the growth and development of our produce. The Hunger Gap runs from January to May, utilising produce that has been preserved while at its best. Time of Abundance, which runs from June to September, is when summer produce is at its best. During the preserving season from October to December, we preserve what we can while fresh produce is still coming from the soil.

For example, we grow chicory root and harvest in late summer to then preserve it by drying. This helps break down the fibres and when we roast the dried pieces, we increase the flavour which results in a coffee-like substance when blended. Potatoes are grown on the farm throughout most of the year, including the late season Charlotte or Linda potatoes we like to use in the recipe we've chosen to share for this book.

CHICORY ROOT AND POTATO DESSERT

Chicory is a unique and flavoursome ingredient that was traditionally grown in the UK during the world wars as a coffee substitute. We pair it with late season Charlotte or Linda potatoes in this dessert, as the starch and sweetness ratio is perfect.

For the potato mousse

550g garden potatoes

600g whole milk

75g butter

110g sugar

1 ½ leaves of gelatine

600ml whipping cream

For the chicory parfait

90g caster sugar

30g liquid glucose

1 ½ leaves of gelatine

300g whipping cream

90g egg yolks

6g chicory powder

For the chicory caramel

150g caster sugar

75g glucose

5g chicory powder

110g cream, warmed

125g butter

3g sea salt

For the chicory crumble

200g butter

105g dark brown sugar

60g caster sugar

190g plain flour

3 tsp chicory root powder, plus extra for dusting

12g baking powder

6g sea salt

For the potato mousse

Wash and peel the potatoes, then slice them ½cm thick straight into cold water. Dry the slices and place them in a pan with all the ingredients except the gelatine and cream. Cook over a medium heat until the potatoes are tender. Meanwhile, soak the gelatine in cold water for 5 minutes then squeeze out the excess water. Add to the potato mixture, blend for 5 minutes to activate the starch, pour the mixture through a fine metal sieve into a bowl, then cover and leave to chill in the fridge. Whip the cream to medium peaks, then fold it into the potato mixture to form a light mousse.

For the chicory parfait

In a pan, heat the sugar, glucose and 25ml of water to 120°c. Soak the gelatine in cold water for 5 minutes then squeeze out the excess water and whip the cream to soft peaks. Whisk the egg yolks until light then slowly add the syrup to them. Add the gelatine and chicory powder, whisk until cool, then fold in the cream. Transfer the mixture to a small container and leave to set in the freezer for 4 hours alongside a chopping board. When set, cut the parfait into twelve portions on the chopping board and return to the freezer.

For the chicory caramel

Combine the sugar and glucose in a small pan and melt without stirring over a medium heat until you have a dark caramel. Stir the chicory into the warm cream, slowly add the mixture to the caramel, then slowly add the butter while stirring continuously so the caramel emulsifies and you have a smooth mixture. Sprinkle in the sea salt then leave the caramel to cool.

For the chicory crumble

Cream the butter with both types of sugar until the mixture is light and fluffy. Add the remaining ingredients and mix to form a paste. Press this into an airtight container and freeze until solid. Grate the mixture onto a lined or non-stick baking tray, then bake for 7 minutes at 160°c. Remove the tray from the oven, carefully break up the crumble, then return to the oven to cook for another 7 minutes. Leave the cooked crumble to cool and firm up.

To serve

Warm the chicory caramel gently in a pan. Divide the chicory crumble between twelve bowls. Place one portion of parfait on top. Take the potato mousse out of the fridge, fold with a spoon to loosen it slightly and spoon some into each bowl. Dust lightly with chicory powder. As you serve the dessert, pour over the warmed caramel.

PREPARATION TIME: 1 HOUR, PLUS 5 HOURS CHILLING AND FREEZING | COOKING TIME: 1 HOUR | SERVES: 12

BROTHERS FARM AND THE TREHANE BLUEBERRY PYO

· ·

BY DAN BENSON

"We didn't grow up as blueberry farmers, nor did we actively seek it out as a profession. The challenge of looking after and making a living from the oldest blueberry plantation in the UK has come to us in a long and winding story..."

When Josh and I were growing up, I don't think we ever really had blueberries…at least I can't remember them if we did! We didn't grow up as blueberry farmers, nor did we actively seek it out as a profession. The challenge of looking after and making a living from the oldest blueberry plantation in the UK has come to us in a long and winding story…

The plants have been here since the late 1950s, when David Trehane took up an offer of 80 blueberry saplings sent over free of charge from Lulu Island in British Columbia. It became an experiment to see how such 'highbush' blueberry varieties would grow in this country. They grew well and actually thrived on Dorset's sandy acidic soil, and years later thanks to lots of TLC they are still going strong.

The land was run by the Trehanes for 60 odd years until the lease for the PYO field was entrusted to my brother Josh in 2015 who had worked as an employee on the plot for several years, learning the trade. A long time before that, when we were both in our late teens, we came and worked summers here picking blueberries for cash!

The land has always been farmed organically, and since 2018 our fruit has been certified organic by the Soil Association which we are very proud of. We have eight varieties on our 3.5 acre field: Herbert, Ivanhoe, Collins, Berkeley, Earliblue, Coville, Blueray and Bluecrop. The first three are no longer grown commercially and they really do have distinct flavours you'd be very hard pushed to find anywhere else.

As with many soft fruits, the harvest time for blueberries is very short (around 6 to 7 weeks for us) and with that comes many risks… So in a bid to diversify our crop, lengthen our season and appeal to a wider audience of visitors we are now growing cut flowers too which is really taking off. Only in our third season together, we're still cutting our teeth and finding our way through the challenges of growing for a living.

We have inherited a unique plot with heritage and history and while the site itself needs a lot of creative development and hard work, our vision is to turn this old field and its surrounding spaces into a place for people to visit, enjoy and take home what this special piece of land has to offer.

MRS B'S LEMON DRIZZLE & BLUEBERRY CAKE

*The most popular cake in our Blueberry PYO café by a Dorset mile,
made by Dan's wife Cecily!*

For the sponge

260g self-raising flour

260g white caster sugar

260g butter

4 free-range eggs (260g)

2 tbsp warm water

2 lemons, zested

260g frozen blueberries (Ivanhoe or Herbert preferably, but any will do!)

For the drizzle

3 lemons, juiced

1 lemon, zested

50g caster sugar, plus extra for topping

Preheat your oven to 180°c and line a baking tray with greaseproof paper. A tray bake approximately 32cm by 22cm by 5cm should give you 15 servings.

In a large bowl, combine the flour and sugar for the sponge. Add the butter, eggs, warm water and lemon zest then whisk everything together for 1 minute.

Pour the cake mixture into the prepared tray and bake in the preheated oven for 10 to 15 minutes, then take it out of the oven and scatter with the frozen blueberries.

Pop the tray back in the oven for another 10 to 15 minutes, or until the surface is golden brown and a thin knife or skewer comes out clean when poked into the centre of the cake.

Place the lemon juice, zest and sugar in a saucepan and heat gently until all the sugar has melted. Make lots of tiny holes in the top of your cake with a thin knife or skewer, then pour the drizzle evenly over the whole surface. Sprinkle a generous handful of caster sugar over the top to give the cake a little crunch, then leave to cool before cutting into portions and serving.

PREPARATION TIME: 15 MINUTES | COOKING TIME: APPROX. 30 MINUTES | SERVES: 15

BROUGHGAMMON FARM

· ·

BY BECKY COLE

"Since its creation, the farm has become a hub of good food and community with regular events, supper clubs and a growing online sustainable meat box service."

We are a forward-thinking, sustainable farm, nestled just off the north coast of Ireland, a stone's throw from the Giant's Causeway. It's a family-run business with my husband Charlie and I, our two young boys and Charlie's parents. Since its creation, the farm has become a hub of good food and community with regular events, supper clubs and a growing sustainable online meat box service.

The business was created back in 2011 when my husband Charlie returned home from a stint as an assistant land agent. Keen to implement what he'd learnt from this and his agricultural studies, he envisioned a farming ethos that utilised the waste of the dairy industry in the form of veal calves and kid goats. The majority were being put down at birth; this seemed such an unnecessary waste so we set out to rear those animals ourselves for delicious and healthy cabrito kid goat meat.

Using his parents' 50 acres as a base for his ideas, Charlie began with a caravan and a few goats. Rearing them by hand, we hit a wall when he realised his market for the eventual goat meat had fallen through. We then decided to butcher them at home instead, creating a delicious and unusual goat meat burger to test out at the local market. Since then we've branched out into rearing free-range rose veal and also seasonal wild game, and in 2019 we began producing vegetables for our farm shop. When Charlie and I met, we also decided to expand the business online by selling ethical meat boxes. This was a huge turning point for us and allowed us to reach a wider audience. We've now developed a rose veal salami using any surplus meat, and our very popular goat bacon.

The farm itself includes an on-site 'nose to tail' butchery, a farm shop and café, monthly supper clubs, farmers' markets and an award-winning street food business that landed us a British Street Food Award. We also run foraging courses throughout the year, alongside herbalist workshops, seasonal cookery classes, fermenting workshops and more. Every Friday to Sunday we open up our doors to the public for open farm visits.

Over the years the farm has become increasingly regenerative, with concerted efforts being made in maximising biodiversity through new woodlands, hedgerows, ponds and diverse rotations. It also has many eco credentials with our eco-farmhouse and solar panels. Charlie and I, with our united passion for the environment, now have exciting plans for developing an agroforestry community project on the land in the near future.

WINTER FARMHOUSE BRAISED ROAST

Here at the farm we rear bull calves for an ethical take on young beef. Outdoor reared, grazed on our lush Northern Irish grass, the meat has a distinct pink colour which is why it's called rose veal. This braised dish is pure comfort and the perfect recipe for any cut of meat that needs a long and slow cook. We make this recipe regularly in our farmhouse kitchen; it's so easy to throw together and guarantees a classic comfort dish that will hopefully become a favourite for you too.

650g rose veal chuck roast

Olive oil

1 red onion, diced

1 tbsp plain flour

1 tbsp tomato purée

3 carrots, roughly chopped

1 parsnip, roughly chopped

1 leek, chopped into 2.5cm rounds

5 cloves of garlic, sliced into quarters

600ml homemade chicken stock

250ml white wine

Preheat your oven to 180°c. Heat a splash of olive oil in a large ovenproof pan, then place the veal into the oil and let it brown on all sides.

Set the meat aside while you add the diced onion to the pan and cook until softened. Stir in the flour then add the tomato purée, carrots, parsnip, leek and garlic. Place the meat back into the pan.

Pour the stock and wine over the meat and vegetables then bring to the boil. Now reduce the liquid to a simmer, cover the pan with a lid and pop into the preheated oven for 2 hours or until the meat is starting to pull apart easily and the sauce has thickened up.

You can serve this dish with a mound of buttery mashed potatoes for a delicious cosy meal to warm up the coldest of nights.

PREPARATION TIME: 20 MINUTES | COOKING TIME: 2 HOURS | SERVES: 6

BURWASH MANOR FARM

BY MIKE RADFORD

"I immediately set about two things: rewilding the farm (coppicing, gapping up and planting hedges and trees, sowing flower-rich grass margins) and to bring the farm into profit by ridding it of grass weeds, using the best varieties and the best chemistry."

The 400 acres of Burwash Manor were bought by my great grandfather over 100 years ago. I joined my father in 1976, my son joined in 2012 and now the sixth generation plays in the corn and feeds the occasional orphaned calf.

After university and International Voluntary Service in Lesotho, I came back to a farm which had been hit by three severe financial blows and was in dire straits. The farm had suffered from Dutch Elm disease and post-war agricultural policies, hence was substantially treeless and hedge-less. With this in mind, I immediately set about two things: rewilding the farm (coppicing, gapping up and planting hedges and trees, sowing flower-rich grass margins) and bringing the farm into profit by ridding it of grass weeds, using the best varieties and the best chemistry.

However, by the mid-1980s, it was becoming clear that we weren't going to be able to farm our way out of trouble. We needed another, more reliable income stream. Utilising the benefit of the farm's position (close to Cambridge, close to major roads, on the edge of a prosperous village) and a nucleus of farm shop, children's shop and tea room, we converted two redundant farm yards into a 'High Street on the Farm'.

Always looking to make life more complicated for ourselves, in 2000 we took the decision to farm organically (which, along with everything else, involved quadrupling the size of our 'hobby' suckler herd). This decision was taken for a mix of reasons (blind optimism in particular); ideological, as I had long become disenchanted with conventional, chemical farming; conservationist, as 40 acres of desert surrounded by a couple of acres of refuge wasn't really working; and economic, as the budgeted bottom line was at least as good and potentially much better.

20 years later, the wildlife is very happy, the cattle are happy and we're still here, although not sure how happy the bank balance is! The farm shop - now The Larder, a busy delicatessen - the children's toyshop and the café are still at the heart of the fifteen varied retail businesses in the two courtyards.

We're now working towards adding holiday lets to our non-farming activities and towards the Holy Grail of organic farming (for us, anyway): zero tillage. Together, hopefully, they will help insulate us against the present government's apparent notion that farming is an industry Britain no longer needs.

BURWASH LARDER

MEATBALLS IN TOMATO SAUCE

This is the recipe that we use in The Larder for our meatball sub sandwiches, but there are any number of variations on the theme; you could use 100% beef or any ratio of pork to beef, and they'll team with any carbs (couscous, quinoa, rice, pasta, noodles, potatoes) or none (finely chopped cauliflower, for example) with gravy, apple sauce, onion marmalade, redcurrant or cranberry jelly, topped with fennel seeds, chilli flakes, or oregano. We're always keen for customers to tell us what works for them!

500g sausage meat (we obviously prefer our own Burwash reared meat!)

1 onion

Knob of butter

2 cloves of garlic

500-700g passata (1 jar)

Salt and pepper, to taste

Dash of Tabasco, if that's your thing

Preheat the oven to 180°c and grease a deep-sided baking tray. Squeeze the sausage meat into a large mixing bowl. Using your hands, shape the mixture into around 20 small balls, each about the size of a gobstopper. Place these a few centimetres apart on the prepared tray and bake in the preheated oven for 10 minutes.

Meanwhile, slice the onion into half centimetre strips and fry gently in the butter. Finely chop the garlic and add to the onion when it has softened. Fry until soft and on the verge of caramelising. Pour the passata over and reduce to a simmer. Add seasonings to taste.

After the 10 minute baking time, shake the meatballs on the tray and pour the sauce over the top, mixing well. Add 50ml of water and put the tray back in the oven for 10 to 15 minutes until the meatballs are cooked through.

Find your crusty bread and grated cheddar cheese, or prepare your pasta and Parmesan, or make some quinoa and salad…whatever you fancy to accompany them!

PREPARATION TIME: 20 MINUTES | COOKING TIME: 20 MINUTES | SERVES: 4

CALDECOTE MANOR FARM

BY SAM TOPHAM

"We currently have 15% of our farm in conservation which hugely benefits all red list species such as linnets, yellow hammers, corn buntings, lapwings and many others, but also improves the habitat for game birds. Walking around the farm is a bird watcher's dream!"

Caldecote Manor Farm is an arable farm in Cambridgeshire with an emphasis on conservation, biodiversity, game management and diversification. Our family has been farming in the area since 1550 and at Caldecote Manor Farm for three generations. We are very much a family farm: I run the day to day workings of the estate, the arable side of the business is under a contract farming agreement, my mum Janice does the bookkeeping and my sister Louise helps out between looking after her young children and working as a vet. We employ a gamekeeper who also helps to run other parts of the business such as Top Storage, a new diversification project providing secure self-storage.

We are passionate about efficient farming linked with achieving environmental net gain and enhancing the biodiversity of the land within our control. We currently have 15% of our farm in conservation which hugely benefits all red list species such as linnets, yellow hammers, corn buntings, lapwings and many others, but also improves the habitat for game birds. Walking around the farm is a bird watcher's dream! Another area of habitat improvement that we are concentrating on includes woodland restoration, with the by-products going into a biomass boiler to replace the use of burning fossil fuels to heat our buildings. We are also restoring a 17th century water meadow to alleviate the effects of flooding, as well as improving the wetland habitat for wildfowl and reducing soil erosion.

The recipe we are sharing features an extremely underused meat product in the UK. Game meat from pheasants and partridge contains more protein than chicken and less fat. Welfare standards tend to be higher as the birds are effectively free to roam the countryside. Pheasants and partridge are released into our woodlands in June or July, and from that point onwards the birds are wild and able to feed on natural food products such as insects, berries and cereals. During the shooting season (September to February) only 40% of the birds we release are taken, leaving the rest to populate the surrounding hedgerows and woodland. The game is then either processed by ourselves or sent to a butcher to be turned into all sorts of different meals, providing local employment and establishing environmentally-friendly habitat in the process.

Despite the challenges that farmers face, we couldn't imagine life away from our farm. We feel very fortunate to live in such a scenic and secluded location, surrounded by woodlands and an array of wildlife.

PHEASANT AND ASPARAGUS BAKE

During shooting season this dish is a firm favourite at the shoot lunches, especially as we always use our own birds. It's equally delicious with partridge, turkey or chicken. – Janice Topham and Louise Santry

2 sticks of celery

1 carrot

1 onion

8 pheasant breasts

1 bay leaf

A few parsley stalks

1 can of asparagus

50g butter

75g plain flour

500ml stock

100ml milk

295ml tin of condensed chicken soup

200ml crème fraiche

1 tbsp wholegrain mustard

2 tbsp chopped parsley

For the topping

25g butter

5 or 6 slices of bread

Make the stock the day before. Roughly chop the celery, carrot and onion. Arrange the pheasant breasts snugly in a casserole dish with the bay leaf and parsley stalks on top. Season with salt and pepper, then cover all the meat and veg with cold water. Bring to the boil and then simmer for 1 and a half to 2 hours until the pheasant breasts are very tender. Leave to cool completely in the liquid, then measure out 500ml of the stock to use in the dish.

When the pheasant breasts are cool, cut each of them into four or five pieces and lay them out in an ovenproof dish. Cut the asparagus into thirds and place on top of the pheasant breasts.

In a separate pan, melt the butter and then stir in the flour to make a paste. Gradually add the stock, milk and chicken soup. Simmer until the sauce has thickened. Remove the pan from the heat and add the crème fraiche, mustard and parsley.

Season the sauce to taste, then pour it over the pheasant breasts and asparagus. Gently mix everything together.

For the topping

Turn the bread into breadcrumbs by whizzing the slices in a food processor. Melt the butter in a pan and add the breadcrumbs. Mix until well combined. Pour the topping over the pheasant and asparagus mixture.

Bake in a preheated oven at 180°c for around 30 minutes. Best served with vegetables and either new or baked potatoes.

PREPARATION TIME: 1 DAY | COOKING TIME: 30 MINUTES | SERVES: 6-8 PEOPLE

CALDECOTT'S

· ·

BY ROBERT CALDECOTT

"We are proud to remain a family business with long-serving, committed staff. As for me, I am just incredibly lucky to spend every day doing something I truly love."

I have always been happy on the farm and I could pluck a turkey at five years of age. I am sure I did want Santa to call at Christmas, but the best bit was helping out with the turkey production.

My father Les and uncle Pete first produced turkeys in the 1950s as they saw a niche market, and the village of Wythall in Worcestershire is very near the county border with the City of Birmingham. They had many years of success but the rise of the supermarkets and their impending retirement meant the business was wound down.

I ventured into egg production for a while, but in 1993 I decided to resurrect the Caldecott Christmas turkey. I could see that the market for traditionally reared local produce was growing consistently, and butchers who had traded with my dad couldn't find a turkey to meet their expectations. My first Christmas production was just 2,500 turkeys: as a business we believe in organic growth and now, almost three decades later, we produce some 60,000 turkeys and as a result of my commitment and passion I was awarded UK Poultry Farmer of the Year in 2016.

The traditional methods I picked up from Dad continue but are complemented by exceedingly high welfare and hygiene procedures, independently inspected to ensure we meet the very highest standards from our own licenced premises. Everything is done in-house which gives me total control. We nurture our day old chicks and poults, then grow our turkeys to maturity with local farmers who all uphold our ethics. A local farmer helps with transporting the flocks from our farms to our processing plant, and a local farming contractor takes our poultry muck away.

The Caldecott family moved to Wythall in 1933 and although it is no longer a small village, we are proud to remain a family business with long-serving, committed staff. As for me, I am just incredibly lucky to spend every day doing something I truly love.

CREAMY JERUSALEM ARTICHOKE AND PARSNIP SOUP

After all the hustle and bustle of December I am renowned for falling asleep too early on Christmas Day. Comfort food is essential for my well-being and this dish is just that. But you don't have to be a turkey farmer to enjoy this. – Robert Caldecott

For the Caldecott Farm Turkey stock

1 turkey carcass

3 bay leaves

1 sprig of thyme

4 peppercorns

1 stick of celery, roughly chopped

1 carrot, roughly chopped

1 white onion, roughly diced

For the soup

Knob of butter

1 white onion, finely chopped

1 stick of celery, finely chopped

1 sprig of thyme

450g Jerusalem artichokes, peeled and diced

200g (about 1 large) parsnip, peeled and diced

1 litre turkey stock (see above)

100ml crème fraiche

Salt and pepper

3 rashers of streaky bacon (optional)

For the Caldecott Farm Turkey stock

Break the turkey carcass into a few pieces so you can fit the whole thing in a large stockpot. Add the bay, thyme, peppercorns, celery, carrot and onion. Fill the pot with enough cold water to cover the carcass by 2 to 3cm. Slowly bring the water to a simmer and reduce the heat to low, then skim off any scum that may form on top (this is impurities from the carcass).

Cover the pot and continue cooking the stock on a low heat for 4 hours. Remove from the heat and discard any bones and vegetables, strain the liquid through a sieve then allow it to cool before leaving the stock in the fridge until set. Skim off the lighter coloured fat that will have formed on top, and your stock is ready to use for the soup.

For the soup

Melt the butter in a large high-sided pan then add the onion, celery and thyme. Sauté over a low heat until softened; this should take about 5 minutes.

Add the diced artichoke and parsnip, cover and allow to gently sweat for 10 minutes. After this time, heat up the stock and add it to the pan. Put the lid back on and simmer gently for 20 minutes until the vegetables are soft. Stir in the crème fraiche and season to taste.

If you want to include them, toast some hazelnuts and top each bowl of soup, then finish with some chopped parsley

Cook's Tip

The stock will form a jelly consistency when cooled – this is the gelatine from the bones forming – but when heated it will return to liquid form. The stock can be kept in the fridge for up to a week, or frozen for 1 month. You can use the stock for the bases of soups, gravy, for poaching poultry or making risottos.

PREPARATION TIME: 10 MINUTES | COOKING TIME: 4 HOURS 30 MINUTES | SERVES: 4

CASTLE FARM

· ·

BY CAROLINE ALEXANDER

"The more I've got to know the farming community over the years, the more I've gained respect for their hard work, multi-skilled entrepreneurialism and deep, unsentimental understanding of how the countryside works."

Some people are just happier leading the outdoor life; there's something about being in tune with the seasons…and feeling comfortable in wellies! The more I've got to know the farming community over the years, the more I've gained respect for their hard work, multi-skilled entrepreneurialism and deep, unsentimental understanding of how the countryside works.

The Alexander family has always enjoyed following its own path, with a passion for ensuring that what was successful for the farm business was also beneficial to the landscape. Back in the 1890s a dairy herd was moved down from Scotland by train to start a farm in Kent. As time went on, the farm expanded and tried new enterprises. In the 1980s a retail outlet was developed, The Hop Shop, which dries hops and flowers for interior decoration and sells the farm's own beef, apple juice and pumpkins. The shop is now open throughout the year with a loyal customer following for its local foods and seasonal gifts.

Since planting began in 2000, Castle Farm has become the biggest lavender farm in the UK, producing essential oils, cut bunches, toiletries and food essences as well as taking thousands of visitors on summer tours. The views are spectacular! People visit us from all over the world, but a working farm is still at the heart of what we do: growing traditional arable crops of wheat and barley and an orchard of heritage apples, raising beef cattle on the water meadows and restoring farm buildings. We've won a number of awards over the years but five gold medals at Chelsea Flower Shows and the Farmers' Weekly Diversification Farmer of The Year awards were our proudest achievements.

Now the next generation are involved, different skills and personalities help diversify the farm still further. From practical energy to skills in PR, photography, chemistry, retail design, online sales and event planning, everyone contributes. And, of course, there's a passion to do things well because this is the family home and livelihood. We never know what's around the corner but are always open to new ideas. Our incredibly successful lavender and hop Sleepy Scent products came from a simple concept of combining our signature products, and the customer response has been incredible.

Likewise, experimenting with our unique Lavender Food Essence has led to a range of delights from our local artisan creators including ice creams, cakes, chocolates, preserves and leaf teas. Our lavender shortbread recipe is just a taster!

LAVENDER SHORTBREAD

A simple recipe for delicately flavoured, melt-in-the-mouth shortbread. Perfect for a relaxing afternoon tea. – Caroline Alexander

200g plain white flour

Pinch of fine sea salt

40g ground rice flour

75g caster sugar, plus extra for decorating

175g unsalted butter, from a chilled 250g block

1 heaped tsp Castle Farm Culinary Lavender Flowers

5-10 drops Castle Farm 'Hot' Lavender Essence

Sift the flour and salt into a bowl and stir in the ground rice flour and sugar. Take your butter from the fridge, and while your bowl is on the weighing scales, grate in 175g of butter from the block. Sprinkle in the lavender flowers and add the drops of lavender essence. Work it all quickly into the flour until the mixture resembles fine breadcrumbs.

Press the shortbread dough gently into a 20cm square baking tin and level out the top. Chill in the fridge for about an hour.

Heat the oven to 140°c and bake the shortbread for 40 minutes until light golden. Remove from the oven and prick all over with a fork, then mark into 20 pieces, cutting right through to the bottom of the tin. Dust the top with caster sugar, then leave the shortbread to cool before removing it from the tin.

Chef's Tip: pressing the shortbread into the tin is the key to getting the right consistency. If the mixture is too hard, the biscuits will set like concrete, but too soft and they will be very crumbly! Firmly pressing another tray on top of the first one is usually the best way to get it right.

PREPARATION TIME: 15 MINUTES, PLUS 1 HOUR CHILLING | COOKING TIME: 40 MINUTES | MAKES ABOUT 20

DAYLESFORD

···

"What began as a simple passion for real food and a desire to feed our children better has grown into Daylesford as we know it today; one of the most sustainable organic farms in the UK."

At Daylesford, our aim is to tread as lightly as we can on this planet, nourishing and preserving the health of the land for future generations. What began as a simple passion for real food and a desire to feed our children better has grown into Daylesford as we know it today; one of the most sustainable organic farms in the UK. We have two farms – one in the Cotswolds and another in Wootton, Staffordshire – which are both certified organic.

All of our crops and animals are grown and reared according to the seasons and without the use of artificial chemicals or antibiotics. While we rely on these traditional methods of farming, new technology is also enabling us to become smarter in the way we operate, such as checking the health of our animals or powering our farm with solar energy.

We also have five farm shops which sell our organic produce and artisan homeware and each serves breakfast, lunch and dinner, all freshly prepared by our in-house chefs. We open our Cotswolds farm twice a year for festivals, teach a variety of workshops at our award-winning cookery school and regularly host craft workshops and many more types of events. Bamford Wellness Spa and Daylesford Farm Cottages provide luxury retreats on our Cotswolds farm alongside our own bakery, creamery, smokehouse and kitchens.

On our Staffordshire farm, we are very proud to have the first and largest red deer herd certified organic by the Soil Association. The animals are free to roam our lush organic pastures, maturing slowly and naturally as they would in the wild, which is why our organic venison is only available during autumn and winter months; a true seasonal highlight. When it comes to our produce, we own the entire story from start to finish, including our own organic hatchery and abattoir. An incredibly passionate team make this possible, from our founder Carole Bamford to our teams on our farms, in our farm shops and in our offices.

We are lucky to have received over 280 awards for our farming practices and our food. Most recently, we were awarded the Supreme Champion award at the Royal Three Counties Show in 2019 for our organic Aldestrop cheese. Being recognised for what we do is extremely rewarding, as we care deeply about farming to the highest standards we can achieve.

VENISON, PORT AND BAY CASSEROLE

This warming casserole celebrates our organic venison, farmed organically on our Staffordshire estate where our deer enjoy a life as wild as possible. Our venison is a nutritious, lean meat and pairs perfectly with root vegetables and winter greens.

For the casserole

Splash of oil

1kg venison haunch, diced

400ml Port

4 bay leaves

2 sprigs of fresh thyme

50g butter

100g streaky bacon, sliced

2 sticks of celery, chopped

1 clove of garlic

300g shallots, peeled

1 tbsp flour

600ml beef stock

Salt and pepper

200g button mushrooms

250g pack of cooked chestnuts

1 tsp English mustard

For the parsnip purée

750g parsnips, peeled and chopped

500ml milk

1 bay leaf and 4 peppercorns

50g butter

Pinch of nutmeg

For the greens

30g butter

1 small savoy cabbage, shredded

Fresh horseradish, grated

For the casserole

Preheat the oven to 160°c or 140°c fan. Heat a little oil in a frying pan and brown the venison in batches, transferring it into a large casserole dish as you go. Deglaze the frying pan over a medium heat by pouring in the Port, bay leaves and thyme. Bring to the boil, scraping everything off the base of the pan, and simmer for 2 minutes. Pour everything into the casserole dish over the meat.

Heat the frying pan again and add the butter, bacon, celery, garlic and shallots. Fry for 10 minutes, until the bacon is golden and slightly crispy and the vegetables have softened. Add the flour and stir for 1 minute. Pour in the stock. Once simmering, transfer the sauce into the casserole dish.

Add salt and pepper, bring to the boil and then place the casserole in the oven for 1 hour. After this time add the button mushrooms, chestnuts and mustard then return it to the oven for another hour.

For the parsnip purée

In the meantime, place the chopped parsnips in a saucepan with the milk, bay leaf and peppercorns. Bring it to the boil then simmer very gently for 12 minutes until the parsnip easily breaks under the back of a fork. Drain, reserving the milk. Place the cooked parsnip in a blender with the butter, nutmeg and a little of the milk. Whizz until you have a very smooth purée, adding more of the warm milk if needed.

For the greens

Heat the butter in a large frying pan and add the shredded cabbage along with 100ml of water. Fry for 5 minutes until wilted but still bright green. Add a little fresh horseradish, then season with salt and pepper to taste.

To serve

Once the casserole is ready, remove the bay leaves and thyme sprigs. Divide between bowls with parsnip purée and greens to accompany each helping.

EASTBROOK FARM

· ·

BY HELEN BROWNING

"I wanted to farm in a way that was more in tune with nature, and gave farm animals the chance of a good life, one where they could express their innate behaviours."

Farming's in my blood, and from the age of eight, that's what I wanted to do. I grew up at Eastbrook Farm, 1350 acres which runs from the top of the Marlborough Downs in North Wiltshire down to the heavy clay land of the Vale of the White Horse. We're Church of England tenants, and my father, Bob Browning, came here in 1950. Following my degree in Agricultural Technology at Harper Adams in 1986, I took over the reins on the farm; I was only 24, so it was a bold move by my father, especially as I was already set to kick over the traces.

I had been concerned about the impacts of modern farming since my teens. I could see the wildlife vanishing, as hedges were removed for ever larger machinery, and increasing volumes of chemicals became the norm. I wanted to farm in a way that was more in tune with nature, and gave farm animals the chance of a good life, one where they could express their innate behaviours. I became interested in organic farming, and spent a year as a research student on the first government funded comparative trial, looking at the differences between organic and chemical farming methods.

I wanted to continue this investigation when I took over Eastbrook. We still had a wide range of enterprises: two dairies, dairy-bred beef, sheep and arable crops, so it was relatively easy to make the switch to organic across all our acres, which we did by 1994. It caused a bit of a stir at the time, as one of the largest tenanted farms to become organic which also happened to be run by a young woman. I soon got involved in agri-politics too, serving on various committees and commissions, and started my long relationship with the Soil Association, where I have been CEO for the last nine years.

Today the farm has a new dairy parlour at the foot of the downs, run by my daughter Sophie (who is also a vet) and her husband, Dai. We still have beef, arable crops and our famous Saddleback pigs, which supply the pork for the Helen Browning's Organic brand. My partner Tim runs HB's Royal Oak, a boutique hotel and dining pub in Bishopstone, and our Chop House in Swindon. Guests can take farm safaris, book photography hides, forage and walk the farm. We are still experimenting, particularly with agroforestry, combining trees with crops and livestock. It's a gloriously busy, sometimes chaotic place. Do come to visit!

HELEN'S ORGANIC PICK AND MIX DINNER

· ·

At home, we live out of our wonderfully random organic veg box, so this is the way I cook, with whatever is around depending on the season. It's fast, healthy and easy food that you can experiment with and adapt to your liking for vegetarians, vegans or carnivores.

Some form of carbs (such as lentils, pasta, diced potato, brown rice) or tinned pulses

Olive oil, onions, garlic, assorted organic vegetables (whatever you have to hand)

Chillies, ginger or other spices that take your fancy

A dash of rice wine vinegar, lemon juice or similar

Your choice of organic meat or other protein, such as sliced pork tenderloin, beef strips, cottage cheese, fried egg (optional)

Possibly something yummy like pesto, harissa, tomato purée or pasta sauce

Greens such as spinach, chard, spring cabbage

Fresh herbs, roughly chopped or torn

Crumbled feta cheese

Put tonight's carb choice (such as lentils, pasta, diced potato, brown basmati rice) into a saucepan of boiling water, with salt or stock if you like. Stir occasionally to prevent sticking and drain when cooked. Alternatively, use a tin of cooked pulses, like black eyed or kidney beans, if you want to save even more time and washing up.

Meanwhile, gently fry chopped onions and garlic in olive oil or another preferred fat, in a big, high-sided frying pan. Chop up a big mound of whatever veg you have around, starting with anything more solid like cauliflower, winter cabbage or carrots that need more cooking time so you can get these into the pan first. I chop tough stuff fairly small, but you could leave the pieces bigger and parboil them with your carbs if al dente veg isn't your thing.

Add any spices you like, and fresh flavourings such as finely chopped ginger or chillies, and stir intermittently to get them cooked evenly. If you have minimised your use of oil, and tomatoes aren't part of the veg mix (these add moisture) then add a dash of liquid at this point such as rice wine vinegar, lemon juice, red wine or even water.

If you are including some meat, get that sizzling now in a separate pan. Pork tenderloin medallions or strips of beef will only need 5 minutes on a medium-high heat.

Once the veg is almost as soft as you would like it to be (usually after about 10 minutes of cooking) stir in your cooked and drained carbs, plus any more spices or sauces you fancy such as pesto, harissa, or a tomato sauce of some kind. Stir everything together while chopping up any greens such as spinach, chard or spring cabbage. Add these into the mix. A minute before serving, scatter in some fresh herbs if you have them and the crumbled feta cheese.

If you have used meat that isn't in bite-size pieces, it's best to serve the meal on a plate, but otherwise everything can go into a lovely big bowl, with only a fork required. A dollop of mayonnaise on top can go down well. Eat as much as you want, and then any leftovers will reheat wonderfully for a quick tasty lunch or side dish.

PREPARATION TIME: APPROX. 20 MINUTES | COOKING TIME: APPROX. 20 MINUTES (WHILE YOU PREP) |
SERVES: AS MANY AS YOU WANT! JUST USE YOUR COMMON SENSE FOR QUANTITIES, DEPENDING ON NUMBERS AND APPETITES.

ENGLISH FARM

BY ROBERT LAYCOCK

"Longhorn cattle thrive on pasture, and those at English Farm are reared the old-fashioned way: always in the open air, on a diet of succulent grasses, meadow herbs and flowers, just as nature intended."

In the 1780s, Robert Bakewell pioneered the "champagne" of beef. He set out to create the first breed of cattle to "represent the roast beef of old England forever and aye". The English Longhorn is proof of his success. Much bigger and broader in the chest than the more commercial and easier-to-handle Angus and Herefords, their horns can span more than five feet. A breeding heifer often weighs three quarters of a ton. These cattle thrive on pasture, and those at English Farm are reared the old-fashioned way: always in the open air, on a diet of succulent grasses, meadow herbs and flowers, just as nature intended.

Our approach recreates the Longhorn's natural habits. This means that despite their fearsome size, our cows live in stress-free family groups and are incredibly easy-going. Calves stay with their mothers for as long as possible and can be over several hundred kilograms before weaning. The result of all this attention to nature is spectacular beef of mouth-watering deliciousness.

Over the last century, as industrial processes have taken hold of food production, many farmers have been forced to prioritise efficiency over quality. Most beef is produced in ways that take a heavy toll on the planet. The vast majority of cows are confined indoors for at least half of the year and fed a high-energy diet entirely unsuited to their evolutionary needs. The plants used to feed them are grown intensively in ways that deplete soils and contribute to global warming. This approach isn't just bad for the planet. It's a defective way to produce food, and the proof's in the taste.

Farmers have been rearing livestock at English Farm for nearly 1,000 years. In 2016, we challenged ourselves to reimagine what a modern farm could be. The result is a focus on the highest ethical standards in the service of two goals: environmental stewardship and fabulous, nutrient-dense flavour.

At English Farm, we don't take from the environment. We give back. Over generations, our herd fertilises the pastures that capture sunlight, water, nitrogen and carbon from the atmosphere. An ecosystem full of birds, bees and butterflies flourishes. This makes for a carbon-negative cow paradise where a glorious herd of Longhorns, permitted to live and eat as nature intended, live happy lives before landing on your table.

RIBEYE TARTARE

· ·

This raw meal is a phenomenal way of enjoying beef raised with utmost care. Our aged ribeye of subtle textures, rich grass-fed fats and delicate notes of flavour is ideal. A tantalising hit of compelling, enriching Longhorn perfectly seasoned with umami is a dish not easily forgotten.

400g English Farm ribeye steak (substitute with fillet for an extra special treat if you'd rather)

6 small capers

2-3 cornichons

½ large shallot

Few leaves of fresh parsley, without stalks

Pinch of sea salt

Crushed black peppercorns

Dash of Tabasco sauce, to taste

Dash of Worcestershire sauce, to taste

2 fresh organic free-range egg yolks

2-4 slices of organic sourdough

For obvious reasons as the ingredients are raw, freshness and food hygiene are critical. Ask us or your butcher for freshly cut ribeye. Tell us that you plan to eat it raw and only use it on the day of purchase for this dish.

Dice rather than mince your ribeye. After the steak is trimmed of any external fat, cut into 0.5cm thick slices with a sharp knife. You will probably get about three slices. Then cut each slice into 0.5cm strips. Dice roughly but try to aim for 0.5cm cubes. A little variation here allows for a better texture. Take a moment to try a piece without any seasoning to understand the flavour basis of this dish. The point here is that the better the beef, the fewer additions you need to enjoy the delicate balance of flavours. Experiment with more or less seasoning according to personal preference.

Separately dice the capers, cornichons and shallot as finely as you can by hand. Don't blend them. Keep them to one side for the moment. Chop the fresh parsley finely.

Put the beef in a bowl deep enough to take all the ingredients, make a little hollow in the middle and add all the diced ingredients and the parsley. Add a small pinch of sea salt and some cracked pepper then, using two forks, gently mix together until the beef is coated with the seasoning. Taste. If you would like to add more flavour at this point, add spice with a few dashes of Tabasco and Worcestershire sauce. Bind the tartare together with one of the egg yolks.

Toast your sourdough. Plate up the tartare with a serving ring or just spoon it carefully into the centre of a generous dish. Place the other egg yolk carefully on top and serve with the toast on the side for a memorable treat.

PREPARATION TIME: 12 MINUTES | SERVES: 2

ESSINGTON FARM

BY RICHARD SIMKIN

"We take great pride in farming using traditional principles with an emphasis on top quality, high welfare meat from our free-range livestock...We prioritise our animals' welfare and give them the best life possible while on our farm."

The Simkin family has been farming in Essington since 1892 and we've been retailing quality, home-grown produce since that date. As a family who have farmed for many generations in Essington, we're truly passionate about offering local food for the local community.

We grow many of our own fruit and vegetables, so it's often the case that our produce is less than an hour old before it appears on the shelves in our farm shop. One of the things that we are well-known for is our Pick Your Own (PYO) fields. We started our PYO in 1978 and are probably the only one left out of around eight that used to operate in our local area. Despite the struggles that other PYOs have faced, our fields seem more and more popular each year with families visiting us to pick their own strawberries, raspberries, plums, and more: in recent years our pumpkins especially have proven extremely popular!

Our award-winning butchery and deli, which we stock with home-produced or locally supplied meat, is also growing in popularity. We take great pride in farming using traditional principles with an emphasis on top quality, high welfare meat from our free-range livestock. All of our pigs, for example, have the freedom to roam outside, root in the soil for food and wallow in the mud to keep cool, making for very happy and healthy pigs. Not only are our pigs content, the result of such a lifestyle is a top quality pork product with excellent flavour and texture.

We also have a suckler herd of pedigree Hereford cattle. The Hereford cow is one of the most famous of the traditional British beef breeds with its distinctive white face and brown and white body. Unlike many modern continental breeds, Herefords are known for their ability to fatten off grass without the need for supplementary feed. As well as having an exceptional flavour, grass-fed beef is a good source of health, providing omega 3 oils and conjugated linoleic acid.

We prioritise our animals' welfare and give them the best life possible while on our farm, and this principle was highly praised by judges at The Butcher's Shop of the Year Awards where we were awarded the winners in the 'Farm Shop of the Year' category in 2019. While our traditional farming practices may not be the most intensive, these methods are good for the environment, good for animal welfare and good for the customer.

FAMOUS PUMPKIN SOUP

· ·

Pumpkin picking in October is always an extremely popular event at the farm. With all the excitement of PYO pumpkins, people forget that it is a vegetable and they are delicious to eat! Our famous pumpkin soup is a favourite treat for many of our customers.

450g potatoes

1 medium pumpkin

1 small onion

450g carrots

200ml olive oil

1.7 litres vegetable or chicken stock

1 bay leaf

285ml single cream

¼ tsp ground or freshly grated nutmeg

Peel and dice the potatoes, pumpkin, onion and carrots.

Fry the diced potatoes, pumpkin flesh, onion and carrots in olive oil for a few minutes.

Add the stock and the bay leaf, then simmer for about 30 to 40 minutes, until the vegetables are tender.

Liquidise the soup to your preference then stir in the cream and nutmeg.

Serve in bowls with fresh bread on the side.

Tip: The seeds from the pumpkin can be toasted and sprinkled on top just before serving if you like.

PREPARATION TIME: 30 MINUTES | COOKING TIME: 40-50 MINUTES | SERVES: 12

SCHOOL FARM

BY KATY LOWE

"When you're not feeling your best, nothing drags you out of bed in the morning quite like a herd of cows that need feeding, makes you as happy as seeing a calf being born (even at 3am) or puts a smile on your face like watching the cows skip out to grass in the spring."

There has never been any other way in which I could picture my life than farming at School Farm. Times spent here as a family are truly my fondest memories of childhood. Having spent eight years away at boarding school, studying for a degree in Politics and working in finance, the farm really was where I felt I belonged and I was immensely happy to return in 2014. My father had worked tirelessly with my mother's support throughout the years and I was so excited to join him and continue the dairy farming business he had so passionately begun. However, in October 2014, Dad died unexpectedly and I found myself running the farm on my own at the age of 24.

I farm a herd of 130 dairy cows, producing organic milk for Belton Farm who produce cheese in Whitchurch, and rear all my own youngstock. In recent years we have modernised the farm hugely with a brand new cubicle shed, slurry storage, calf pens and, most excitingly, by installing robotic milking machines which has been life changing.

My parents converted to organic farming methods in 2000 and in the past 20 years our commitment to this has only increased. I believe passionately that my job as a farmer is not simply to push for the highest yields and greatest profits but to be a custodian of both the land and environment.

I am now married to James and we have a daughter, Beatrice. James is not from a farming background but gets roped in to help many evenings and weekends and has thrown himself into the farming life. Mum also now has a partner, John, who as an ex-dairy farmer has quickly become my right hand man and I'm not sure what we'd do without him.

The past six years have thrown up many challenges and life has not been plain sailing, but the relentlessness of farming has at times been a blessing. When you're not feeling your best, nothing drags you out of bed in the morning quite like a herd of cows that need feeding, makes you as happy as seeing a calf being born (even at 3am) or puts a smile on your face like watching the cows skip out to grass in the spring. Through all its ups, downs, twists and turns, farming really is for the most part a pleasure and a privilege.

CREAMY PORK MEDALLIONS

· ·

This is a great dish for autumn and winter, showcasing pork at its absolute best. It's quick and simple to prepare but makes an impressive dinner party main. If medallions are hard to find, buy pork tenderloin and slice to suit.

6 (about 300g) pork fillet medallions

6 rashers of smoked streaky bacon

Salt and pepper

1 tbsp oil

1 large apple, peeled, cored and sliced into wedges

50ml cider

50ml chicken or vegetable stock

50ml double cream

1 tsp wholegrain mustard

Wrap a rasher of bacon around each medallion and season with salt and pepper.

Heat the oil in a pan over a medium to high heat.

Add the medallions and cook for 3 to 4 minutes on each side ensuring the bacon crisps up nicely around the outside. Add the apple to the pan and brown on all sides.

Once the pork is cooked, transfer to a plate, cover with foil and set aside to rest.

Add the cider to the pan with the apples and stir, then add the stock, cream and mustard and simmer until reduced and thickened.

Return the medallions and any juices back to the pan and simmer for a further minute until the pork is heated through, then remove from the heat and serve.

Perfect with honey roast parsnips and creamy mashed potato.

THE FEMALE FARMER

· ·

PAGE 80

FIR FARM

· ·

BY PADDY HOARE

"Our organic methods and innovative practices work in harmony with nature to enhance biodiversity, improve soil fertility and conserve the environment while growing highly nutritious food without diminishing our natural capital."

At Fir Farm, we are working towards creating a fully sustainable, closed-loop farming system. Our organic methods and innovative practices work in harmony with nature to enhance biodiversity, improve soil fertility and conserve the environment while growing highly nutritious food without diminishing our natural capital. Jane Parker, the farm owner, started this regenerative drive about seven years ago, and we are still learning something new every day by always trying to improve.

Since 2013 we have raised our animals on an organic basis, and we are now Pasture for Life registered producers (100% grass fed cattle and sheep) and Soil Association certified producers. We are passionate about animal welfare, so much so that Jane commissioned a team to design and build a mobile abattoir so that our animals, which are all born and raised on the farm, can be slaughtered on site and don't ever have to leave the farm.

We are constantly reviewing our methods in order to reduce our carbon footprint. At present, following an NFU study, our cows are carbon neutral due to our mob grazing system and the fact that they only eat grass produced on the farm. We move the cows onto fresh grass every day, which improves the soil's organic matter, increases grass yield and the number of grazing days in each field, and means the cows are always getting the best quality grass. We are aiming to introduce more renewable energy which includes solar arrays, ground source heat pumps and biomass systems. We are also looking into the viability of a Papa Pump so that our water system on the farm is off grid and requires no electrical pumps.

Our chickens are fed mealworms alongside their main diet, which we produce on the farm using vegetable cuttings dropped off by people from the village, who buy eggs from the end of our farm drive. Our chickens live in eggmobiles, which are chicken huts on wheels with automatic solar-powered doors and slatted floors. This allows us to move the chickens behind the mob grazed cattle, letting them fertilise the grass, forage all over the fields, and provide fresh eggs. Mealworms are high in protein and help the chickens develop a strong gut to fight diseases and parasites, which they eat in the cowpats and thus help to reduce the animal worm burden on the farm. This cyclical system improves the soil, which results in quality grass and, in turn, truly healthy and delicious beef!

RECTORY FARM

RBOSA HEREFORDS

FIR FARM LTD

BEEF SHIN RAGU WITH GREMOLATA

A family favourite at Fir Farm. Beef shin is one of the cheapest cuts and requires patience, but the result – melt-in-the-mouth shreds of meat in a rich sauce – is well worth the wait. A zingy gremolata cuts through the richness and makes it a year-round winner. This freezes brilliantly so double up. – Paddy Hoare

800g Fir Farm beef shin

Splash of olive oil

Sea salt and freshly ground pepper

50g butter, plus an extra knob

2 carrots, grated

2 sticks of celery, finely chopped

2 onions, peeled and finely chopped

4 cloves of garlic

3 anchovy fillets

2 tbsp tomato purée

1 bouquet garni (bay leaves, rosemary and thyme)

300ml red wine

500ml Fir Farm beef bone broth, or good quality beef stock

400g pappardelle pasta

Shaved Parmesan, to serve

For the gremolata

2 lemons, zested and juiced

2 cloves of garlic

Big handful of flat leaf parsley

2 tbsp olive oil

3 anchovy fillets

Preheat the oven to 180°c or 160°c fan. Bring the beef shin to room temperature then pat dry, rub with olive and season generously. Put a casserole dish on the hob to get really hot, then sear the shin for 3 to 4 minutes on each side to brown and seal the meat. Take it out the pan and set aside.

Turn the heat down, melt the butter in the dish then add the carrots, celery and onions. Cook for 5 minutes until softened then add garlic, anchovies, tomato purée and bouquet garni to cook for a minute. Add the wine and turn up the heat to bring it to the boil, then stir in the broth or stock. Place the beef shin back into the dish along with any resting juices. Bring the liquid back to the boil, then put the lid on and pop the ragu into the oven. Reduce the temperature to 160°c or 140°c with fan and cook for 3 hours 30 minutes.

For the gremolata

Put all the ingredients into a food processor and whizz a couple of times to combine everything. Alternatively, place it all on a large board and chop until combined, then add the lemon juice.

Cook the pasta according to the packet instructions in boiling salted water, drain and add the knob of butter.

Shred the beef in the ragu with a couple of forks, taste and season. Serve tossed with the pappardelle and topped with a good drizzle of the gremolata and some shaved Parmesan.

PREPARATION TIME: 30 MINUTES | COOKING TIME: 3½ HOURS | SERVES: 6-8

FULLER'S HILL FARM

BY JOHN JEFFERIES

"The farm is now busy every day of the year and about half of the farm income is now from non-farm activities. But farming and food production is the life blood of my day."

My family have farmed for generations and can be traced back to the mid-1300s on my mother's side and to at least 1750 on my father's side of the family. Maybe that's why my earliest memories are on the farm, and of wishing to farm the land.

Fuller's Hill Farm has been in the family for about 100 years. I took over the management of the farm when I was 22. Since then, I have managed to double the farmed area and expand the business into non-farm activities such as a small airfield on the farm. Over the past 10 years I have redeveloped the redundant Victorian farm buildings into self-catering holiday lets. The farm is now busy every day of the year and about half of the farm income is now from non-farm activities. But farming and food production is the life blood of my day.

Farming has changed so much in my 34 years of experience. The most recent change is the conversion to conservation agriculture (CA). CA is a genre of farming that seeks to use what happens naturally within the environment to reduce the cost of farming while maintaining production levels. At the heart of this is soil health and fertility.

Soil health is promoted by the use of manures, composts, crop residues and cover crops (a crop grown between cash crops). These all seek to promote soil life, principally by providing food for the humble earthworm, of which there are about 20 species in the UK. The earthworms themselves leave residues that are food for other forms of soil life, bacteria and fungi. This whole eco-system improves soil structure, texture and drainage.

All of the above is destroyed by the plough. Inverting the soil kills the earthworms and the drainage they create. The weight of the machinery crushes the soil structure and texture. In CA, crops are planted with a direct drill which places the seed in the ground with minimal soil disturbance. CA also has huge benefits in improving the environment for all indigenous species and frequently reduces the need for fertiliser and pesticides as nature rediscovers its balance.

CA also has huge environmental benefits. We can remove vast amounts of carbon dioxide from the air and lock them away in the soil forever, quicker than a newly planted forest. We farmers can produce food and seek to get the climate back under control.

FIRE BOWL STEAK

· ·

My recipe is a favourite way to cook some fantastic local produce, in this case Hereford beef from the River Gt Ouse flood meadows near Bedford. The rib eye steak is barbecued on the embers of a hot open fire, a method I saw on honeymoon with Jenny in Africa. – John Jefferies

2 côte de bœuf steaks

I shallot

Knob of butter

Splash of brandy

Black peppercorns, crushed (to taste)

Splash of double cream

Salad of your choice

First, visit your local farm shop and order the côte de bœuf steaks. These are trimmed rib-eye steaks on the bone, each about 50mm thick. This is the best cut as it well marbled, tender and flavoursome. I purchase steaks from Woodview Farm Shop. Their beef is raised by a family member on the flood plains of the River Gt Ouse at Gt Barford, so the land is very fertile and grows high quality grass.

About an hour and half before you want to eat, light your fire bowl. Stack it with as many dry logs as possible. If you don't have a fire bowl, you can remove a circle of turf from your lawn, about 60cm in diameter. Dig out about 100mm of soil and make a small bank around the edge. Light your fire in the pit you have just made. Replace the turf the next day and water it well.

At the same time, take your steak out of the fridge so it can warm up to room temperature. During this time you can also make your peppercorn sauce. Finely dice the shallot and fry gently in butter. Add the brandy, crushed peppercorns and double cream. Thicken the sauce over the heat then set aside. Preheat your normal oven to 150°c.

Prepare the salads of your choice. I use locally grown new potatoes garnished with chives and a little mayo alongside a green salad that normally includes coriander and tomatoes from the garden. But a baby leaf salad, basil with mozzarella and tomato or a Waldorf salad will do the job equally well.

When your fire bowl is well lit, after about an hour, knock down the logs so that you have a good 50 to 75mm of glowing hot embers. Simply place the steaks straight on to the embers and cook them for 4 minutes per side. After the steaks are cooked (you might need to clean off the embers) place them in the preheated oven for 20 minutes. Meanwhile, place a few more logs on the fire so you have a focal point for the rest of the evening.

Remove the steaks from the oven and allow them to rest for a couple of minutes. Then just carve off slices of succulent steak and enjoy with your salads, peppercorn sauce and a glass of red wine. I would normally serve this with a good Chilean Carménère or Argentinian Malbec.

PREPARATION TIME: I HOUR 30 MINUTES | COOKING TIME: 30 MINUTES | SERVES: 2-4

TYN LLWYFAN FARM

BY GARETH WYN JONES

"One tweet and Facebook message changed my life. I could have turned my back but decided to invite reporters and journalists onto our farm and share our story with the world."

I am passionate about producing sustainable, seasonal, local food. You've got to look after and respect the land, not rape and pillage it. By managing farmland sustainably, we can continue producing protein without damaging the ecological balance. We have been farming in the Carneddau mountains for over 350 years, and still have rare flora and fauna in abundance, which our Welsh mountain sheep can forage for and in turn produce delicate and subtly flavoured lamb and mutton. I believe it's the best in the world.

We have around 3,500 breeding ewes and 300 head of cattle, as well as chickens, ducks, turkeys for Christmas and bees. By farming the old-fashioned way, we are putting back what we've taken from the land. We also have our own vegetable plot, and so we grow our own seasonal vegetables. It's a family-run business which used to be run by four brothers and their four sons. Today it's a partnership consisting of my father, his brother Uncle Wil and his son Ieuan, then my other cousin Robat, Owen John and myself. Everyone plays their part and our work ethic is all about hard graft and determination.

It's also important that we get out and interact with the public and our customers. To this end, I'm known as the 'Tweeting Farmer'. I think it's vital to bridge the gap between town and country and to educate people. I had that opportunity on the 22nd March 2013: it was early spring and we had a freak snow storm, which hit certain areas of North Wales badly, including us. It was lambing time and we were struck by surprise with the blizzard. I was using social media at the time to connect with family and friends and decided to show the impact the weather can have on our livelihood. One tweet and Facebook message changed my life. I could have turned my back but decided to invite reporters and journalists onto our farm and share our story with the world.

That opportunity allowed us as farmers to show the general public not only the cost of producing food, but also the human, emotional and physical cost. We had so much support it was overwhelming. We have now started to diversify into tourism, and hope to expand on this by providing bespoke tours and experiences on the farm. It is so important to educate the next generation about eating well, sustainability, seasonal food and respecting the environment as part of leading a healthy and happy lifestyle.

MUTTON LOBSGOWS – 'CAWL TYN LLWYFAN'

This is a traditional dish in North Wales and a staple for farmers and the working class, known as 'cawl' further south. Usually made with braising steak, it's just as tasty and more sustainable to use mutton. A wholesome dish that leaves only one pot to clean!
– Rhian and Gareth Wyn Jones

900g lamb neck or 450-675g mutton or braising steaks, cut into good chunks

Splash of olive oil

1 onion, peeled and diced

1.1 litres chicken stock for lamb or beef stock for mutton and beef (preferably homemade or jelly stock pots)

Splash of Worcestershire sauce (optional)

Salt and pepper

4 medium potatoes, cubed

6 long carrots, roughly chopped

½ a turnip

1 or 2 leeks, thinly sliced

For the homemade bread

1 tsp dried yeast

170g wholemeal flour

340g white flour

½ tsp sugar

½ tsp salt

350ml water

Heat a large heavy-bottomed pan, then seal the lamb, mutton or beef in olive oil. Add the onion and cook until soft. Pour in about half of the stock, enough to cover the meat, and bring it to the boil. If you are using mutton, add a dash of Worcestershire sauce to taste. Cover the pan with a lid and leave the meat to simmer for 1 hour.

At this point, add salt and pepper. If you have used neck of lamb, let the mixture cool, skim off the fat, take all the meat off the bone and stir it back into the pan. Place it back on the heat.

Add the chopped potatoes, cook for 5 minutes, and then add the carrots, turnip and the remaining stock. Bring to the boil and simmer for 10 minutes. Taste the stew to check the seasoning, adding more salt and pepper if necessary, then make sure the vegetables are covered with the liquid. You can add more stock if necessary but don't make the stew too runny.

Stir in the sliced leek and cook for 5 to 8 minutes, or until everything is cooked. You can also add a handful of sprouts or peas to cook for the last few minutes. Lobsgows is best eaten the next day when the stew has thickened and flavours have intensified. Serve with homemade buttered bread.

For the homemade bread

You can make this in advance or while the stew is cooking. Mix all the ingredients well then knead the dough for 15 minutes. Cover and leave it to prove for 1 hour in a warm place until doubled in size. Shape into a square loaf and bake the bread in the oven at 180°c for 1 hour.

THE GARLIC FARM

BY NATASHA EDWARDS

"When it comes to garlic, we feel we are veritable experts, from growing to cooking to health benefits and folklore. Each year, up to 30 different varieties of garlic from around the world are trialled at the farm and we are visited by up to 250,000 people at our farm shop and restaurant."

My grandparents first started farming on the Isle of Wight in the 1950s and my grandmother experimented with garlic growing early on in her kitchen garden. When my parents joined the farm in the 1970s, Colin (my father) decided to start growing garlic commercially. Now my husband Barnaby and I are actively running the operations with my father still involved in the arable and land management. My brother Hugo and his wife Mel run the holiday accommodation, and we have a team of up to 70 people throughout the year across our different parts of the business. Everyone plays a key role in keeping the show on the road!

We are a third-generation family business, and our passion is firmly focused on excellent quality garlic production and sourcing, as well as the creation of a whole spectrum of flavours using garlic. We now have over 60 products we produce with garlic at the centre, and have been nominated by Ocado as Britain's Best Supplier. When it comes to garlic, we feel we are veritable experts from growing to cooking to health benefits and folklore. Each year, up to 30 different varieties of garlic from around the world are trialled at the farm and we are visited by up to 250,000 people at our farm shop and restaurant.

Our customers can visit any day of the year to get fully immersed in the garlic experience. We also have a Garlic Festival every August here on the island which is attended up by to 30,000 people over two days. We run lots of other events throughout the year at our shop and restaurant – which is listed in the 2020 Good Food Guide as a Local Gem – as well as offering accommodation on site in our luxury yurts and farm cottages.

Most of our land is under higher level stewardship schemes, meaning that we are following environmental stewardship guidelines. We are committed to using minimum chemical intervention and believe in supporting biodiversity, habitats for wildlife and access for educational purposes. Any visitor to our farm can take walks around our land and access free educational material about how we farm, learning all about the art of growing garlic.

OAK-SMOKED GARLIC DAUPHINOISE

· ·

Smoked garlic is one of our most popular products and works very well with creamy dishes. Garlic bulbs are hot-smoked over oak chippings for up to 48 hours here at our farm on the Isle of Wight. Smoked garlic flavours permeate the creamy potatoes, bringing a unique twist to this classic dish. – Natasha Edwards

1kg waxy firm potatoes, peeled and thinly sliced

1 tsp ground or grated nutmeg

Sea salt and freshly ground black pepper, to taste

6 fat cloves of oak-smoked garlic, peeled

500ml full cream milk (or mix milk with cream)

50g salted butter

Preheat the oven to 190°c. Layer half the sliced potato into an ovenproof dish. Sprinkle over half the nutmeg and a good seasoning of salt and pepper. Grate all the garlic cloves on top. Tip the rest of the potato slices into the dish and spread them out evenly. Season again with salt and pepper, then pour over the milk and cream. Dot small pieces of butter over the top. Bake the dauphinoise in the preheated oven until all the liquid has been absorbed and the top has browned. This usually takes about 1 to 1 and a half hours. Serve alongside a good portion of roasted meat and vegetables.

PREPARATION TIME: 10 MINUTES | COOKING TIME: 1 HOUR 30 MINUTES | SERVES: 6-8

GRAIG FARM ORGANICS

BY JONATHAN REES

"This job is where I can really live out my passion, and animal welfare is at the top of the list. Organic farming, or what I call 'farming how it used to be' is the only way forward."

As a Welsh farmer, life can be a little demanding, especially with lambing just around the corner. Running the farm and the on-farm butchery can take its toll most days, even without the weather playing up on a cold January morning.

But it helps when you love what you do. My day starts at 4:30am with the livestock having to be fed and lambs taken to the abattoir. This is normal and as each job finishes, I remind myself what it's all for, as I am passionate about good produce.

Once all the livestock has been tended to, I am able to fulfil my other passion; processing our wonderful organic produce, whether it's for that perfect Sunday roast or a steak for a romantic candlelit dinner. When we start processing our wonderful produce I start to get hungry, and can't resist putting some aside to take down to the farmhouse later that day, as I know it will taste amazing.

Having processed organic beef, lamb, pork, chicken, game and fish I am involved on both sides of the plate. Many supermarkets have become fixated on profit, which is so sad because we are losing our native breeds to the European breeds as they yield more meat.

I believe it's a pure joy to have been fortunate enough to have been given the chance be a farmer. This job is where I can really live out my passion, and animal welfare is top of the list. Organic farming, or what I call 'farming how it used to be' is the only way forward. It's sustainable and it actually gives more than it takes away.

Recently my farming methods are changing in an attempt to reduce plastic, as it has become clear that this is a major problem. Everything has plastic on it or in it. On one occasion I wrapped my cut of meat in brown paper, and when I delivered the meat to the kitchen table the whole family gathered around to see what treasures I was about to reveal.

It was then I realised that we need to give all our customers the option of meat wrapped in paper, not horrible plastic bags. Let us not forget that meat has only been wrapped in plastic for the last 25 years.

In order to create a better future, I look to the past.

ROAST FORE RIB GLAZED IN
MUSTARD AND HORSERADISH SAUCE

· ·

With slow roasting joints, the nearer you are to the foot or head the more sinew the muscle contains. When sinew is cooked for a long period it turns to jelly, and it is delicious! – Jonathan Rees

1 beef forerib (2 ribs = 3kg)

2 tbsp horseradish

2 tbsp mustard

2 tbsp brown sugar

1 tsp salt

1 tsp pepper

When you are thinking about cooking slow roasts, you never really have to worry about what joint comes into this category, as all meat can be cooked slowly. Shin is the nearest you can get to the foot and therefore the toughest.

I always make up a simple paste of horseradish, mustard, brown sugar, salt and pepper. Coat your joint with the paste, covering it completely.

Place the joint in the oven, set the temperature at 80°c and cook for 15 to 22 hours. Really I am not too worried on time, but it needs to be over 15 hours.

The science behind my method is all about the meat coming up to the temperature as slowly as possible, because moisture evaporates above 100°c and this is why it remains so juicy.

The next day, you should have a joint of meat that is cooked. However, I like my meat crispy and caramelised. In order to do this, you need to take the oven temperature up 220°c but take the joint out first. Once it's up to temperature place the meat back into the oven. All you need to do is brown the meat, which should take 15 to 20 minutes.

Leave it to rest for 10 minutes. Enjoy.

PREPARATION TIME: 10 MINUTES | COOKING TIME 15-22 HOURS | SERVES: 8

HEADY'S FARM

BY RICHARD HEADY

"My family have shared farm life with me, so now I try and share it with the world...I believe that it is so important that we know where our food has come from."

Farming gives me so much job satisfaction. Every day I get to see the rewards of our hard work: the crops and animals growing and the wildlife thriving, and that's why I love it. I grew up on our family farm in Buckinghamshire working with my dad and uncle as I still do today, but with the added joy of my children coming out to join in where they can. My family have shared farm life with me, so now I try and share it with the world, by making short regular farming videos. While busy on the farm I film the job, explaining what we are doing and why, before sharing it to social media @headysfarm. This hopefully helps to bridge the gap between producers and consumers, as I believe that it is so important that we know where our food has come from and how it was produced.

We are lucky that we can beg, borrow or steal most of the ingredients for the recipe that follows, and I am sure it tastes all the better for it. We raise our own beef on grass and barley alone, and find it fits in really well with our arable (crop growing) system. The cattle poo is spread on the fields to improve our soil nutrition which then helps the barley to grow. The barley is then milled on the farm to feed the cattle and the straw (barley stalks) is used as bedding to keep the cattle clean and comfortable while they are inside during the winter.

While most of our beef will end up on a supermarket shelf, we keep one beast back for ourselves to eat and sell as meat boxes. Not to blow our own trumpet, but the beef is always excellent, and I put this down to two points, low stress and good quality diet. The cattle are born and raised on our farm so they get very used to me working with them, resulting in very little stress, and stress hormones have a huge effect on meat tenderness. Secondly, the majority of their diet is grass – just as nature intended – with a little barley to help them fatten, and this is what makes the flavour so great.

Our beef boxes allow us to trade with our neighbours for other fantastic local meat that we don't rear ourselves, like pork. So when the stewing steak and sausages in the recipe are sorted, we then raid my brother's glass house for chillies and tomatoes (the flavour is unbelievable), before heading to my mum's chickens to snatch some eggs.

PIQUE MACHO

This is not your average farmer's dish, but the name translates roughly as food of the strong, so I think it fits farm life pretty well. We stumbled across it in Bolivia; in my terrible Spanish I managed to ask for a taste and we have been hooked ever since! –
Richard Heady

500g stewing steak

400g sausages

3 medium onions

2 cloves of garlic

2 red or yellow peppers

1-2 fresh chillies (or 3 tsp hot chilli powder)

1 stock cube

1 tbsp soy sauce

½ a bottle of local ale

400g fresh or tinned chopped tomatoes

Pinch of salt and pepper

To serve

4 portions of chips or fries

6 eggs

Mayonnaise

Dice the stewing steak and slice the sausages into bite-size pieces. Brown the meat in a hot frying pan. Meanwhile, peel and dice the onion and garlic. Deseed and chop the peppers, then do the same with the fresh chillies, if using.

Add the onion, garlic and peppers to the pan and cook until softened. Then transfer the meat and vegetables to a casserole dish and add the chilli, stock cube, soy sauce, ale, tomatoes and seasoning. Give everything a good stir then place the dish into the oven and cook at 180°c for 2 hours and 30 minutes, topping up the sauce with ale to keep it moist when needed.

While the pique macho cooks, prepare the chips and hard boil the eggs. Serve the spicy beef and sausage stew on top of the chips, topped off with a quartered egg and a swirl of mayonnaise each.

HIRST FARMS

BY RICHARD HIRST

"Without a doubt, farmers have got to take more responsibility for promoting food directly and that's partly why we decided to engage with the public and bring them right onto our land."

I've always wanted to be a farmer, from the moment I could say the word. I feel very privileged to own my family farm, and lucky to be here every day with my wife and children. We grow a range of crops including wheat, barley, sugar beet, potatoes, peas, lettuces and lots more. There's also our flock of 320 ewes, 140 head of cattle and 2000 pigs, plus my wife Katrina and younger daughter Ellie run the livery of 40 horses on site. My grandfather bought the original farm in 1955 and then my father farmed it until I took over in the early 1990s. My son Robert runs the farm these days, and my oldest daughter Fiona does the bookkeeping, so we really are a family enterprise.

We started as a mixed arable farm, but diversified to create our seasonal tourist attraction, which has become really popular and is just as integral to the business. Hirsty's Family Fun Park was the first of its kind for East Norfolk and gives us a chance to explain what we do and where people's food comes from. There's a giant maize maze in summer, a wool festival showcasing sheep shearing, Halloween pumpkin activities, open lambing sessions around Easter time and lots of other fun seasonal stuff throughout the year. It's a great family day out and we're always looking for ways to make the fun park even better. Even more importantly, children have the opportunity to see lambs being born, or realise where those veggies on their plate actually come from, which is very valuable in my eyes.

Without a doubt, farmers have got to take more responsibility for promoting food directly and that's partly why we decided to engage with the public and bring them right onto our land. About 75% of the beef and lamb we raise starts and finishes on the farm, because we sell directly to customers and at the fun park when events are on. Our farming methods are fairly traditional, aiming to grow crops and rear animals that achieve a good balance between quality and yield. For me, it's all about producing great food for people to eat, while protecting the environment. Nearly 10% of our land is set aside for environmental benefits; field margins and corners are left to revert back to nature, wild bird feeding plots provide sustenance over winter, and we plant hedgerows and trees to try and work in harmony with the countryside that gives us our livelihood.

RICHARD'S RICE PUDDING

A really easy pudding to make and a real Hirst favourite. My parents, who are in their 90s, have it every day and so did I when I was I younger. Every family gathering has to have one on the pudding menu! – Richard Hirst

40g butter

100g pudding rice

75g caster sugar

1 litre full-fat milk

150ml double cream

1 tsp vanilla extract or ½ vanilla pod, split lengthways

Pinch of salt

Plenty of freshly grated nutmeg

Preheat the oven to 140°c while you melt the butter in a heavy-based casserole dish over a medium heat. Add the rice and stir to coat. Add the sugar, stirring until it has dissolved. Continue stirring until the rice swells and becomes sticky with the sugar.

Pour in the milk and keep stirring until no lumps remain. Add the cream, vanilla and salt, then bring the mixture to a simmer. Once this point is reached, give the mixture a final stir and grate at least a third of a nutmeg over the surface. Bake for 1 to 1 and a half hours and cover with foil if the surface browns too quickly.

Once there is a thin tarpaulin-like skin on the surface, and the pudding only just wobbles in the centre, it is ready. Serve at room temperature.

PREPARATION TIME: 5 MINUTES | COOKING TIME: 1 HOUR 30 MINUTES | SERVES: 4

THE HOME FARMER

BY BEN SPENCE

"It's nice knowing the cows by name, not just as a number on a screen, and keeping the herd small means we can put their happiness high on the priority list."

We're a small family farm in the beautiful countryside of Wensleydale, selling fresh milk, making cheese and looking after our herd of Friesian cows. Myself and my brother Adam run the business alongside our parents, David and Susan, and my wife Samantha. Our grandparents Harold and Nora Spence bought The Home Farm in 1953 and started producing dairy. Today, there's about 100 head of cattle so we're still a small farm by modern standards, but we do this because it's always been the way to add value and stick with quality over quantity for us.

Just before Christmas 2019, we diversified by creating our own Wensleydale cheese. It's made and matured here on the farm using raw milk fresh from our own cows, and is full of flavour and creamier than most Wensleydale cheeses because the milk is unpasteurised and it's made more slowly to a traditional recipe. Another main focus of the last few years has been significant reinvestment in a new milking parlour and cattle shed. The impetus for this was animal welfare; improving the living standards for our cows is really important. It's nice knowing the cows by name, not just as a number on a screen, and keeping the herd small means we can put their happiness high on the priority list.

The Home Farmer now also has a mobile vending machine which we reckon is probably the first of its kind in the UK. A converted horsebox delivers our milk and cheese to surrounding villages, stopping off at each location on a weekly schedule that gives our neighbours the chance to buy really fresh produce that's incredibly local. It's done well so far, and a couple of nearby supermarkets have added to our list of stockists alongside Wensleydale Creamery where we have long sent the majority of our milk. They now also have our cheese in the lovely deli which was a proud moment.

Adam and I came back to the farm about seven years ago, and Sam joined us a few years after that – our dad thinks we're mad, because we all left different professions to take it on – but we liked the idea of being our own bosses, and for Sam and I it's nice to be around our kids rather than in an office all day. We even had a meeting in our Christmas pyjamas once… In all seriousness though, being a small family farm means we can make animal welfare and quality local produce our main concern, and it's a great way to make a living.

BEN'S 'FEED A FARMER' LASAGNE

· ·

We love hearty family meals at Home Farm and lasagne is one of our favourites. As dairy farmers we always have milk and cheese in the fridge so it's our 'go to' if we can't decide what to have. Farmers are famously always hungry but this never fails to hit the spot! – Ben Spence

1 medium onion

1 red sweet pointed pepper

1 tbsp olive oil

1 tsp garlic purée (or 1 clove of garlic, peeled and crushed)

500g good quality minced beef

2 x 400g tins of chopped tomatoes

Salt and pepper

1 heaped tsp sundried tomato pesto

1 heaped tsp basil pesto

1 tsp hot chilli powder

1 tsp dried Italian herb seasoning

Splash of Worcestershire sauce (or balsamic vinegar)

1 beef stock cube

50g butter

50g plain flour

550ml milk (ideally Home Farmer fresh farm milk!)

100g cheese, grated (we always use our Old Roan Farmhouse Wensleydale)

250g dried lasagne sheets

Preheat the oven to 180°c. You'll need a 22cm by 30cm ovenproof dish.

First, make the lasagne sauce. Peel and finely chop the onion. Halve the red pepper, remove the stalk and seeds then roughly chop. Heat the oil in a large non-stick frying pan on a medium to high heat. Add the onion, peppers and garlic then fry for 4 to 6 minutes, stirring often until softened and lightly coloured. Stir in the minced beef and cook everything for 4 to 5 minutes until the meat is no longer pink. Add the tinned tomatoes and season with salt and pepper.

Stir in the sundried tomato pesto, basil pesto, chilli powder, Italian herbs and Worcestershire sauce or balsamic vinegar. Crumble in the stock cube. Bring to a gentle simmer, cover and cook over a low heat for 20 minutes, stirring occasionally.

While the lasagne sauce is simmering, make the white sauce. Melt the butter in a large saucepan on a medium to high heat. Add the flour and beat it into the butter to make a smooth paste. Slowly pour in the milk and whisk until the paste has dissolved. Keep on the heat, whisking continuously, until you have a smooth sauce. Add half the grated cheese and allow it to melt. Season the sauce with salt and pepper to taste.

Assemble the lasagne. Spoon half of your lasagne sauce into the ovenproof dish. Follow with a layer of lasagne sheets. Pour over half of the white sauce and spread it to cover the lasagne sheets. Add the other half of your lasagne sauce, then follow with lasagne sheets and the remaining white sauce once again. Top with the remaining grated cheese.

Bake the lasagne in the preheated oven for 30 minutes until it is bubbling and golden. Serve with seasonal steamed green vegetables, fresh coleslaw and crunchy garlic bread.

Top Tip: we like to assemble the lasagne earlier in the day where possible and store it in the fridge for a few hours before cooking (it needs 40 minutes in the oven if baking straight from the fridge). This allows the lasagne sheets to soak up the sauce.

PREPARATION TIME: 40 MINUTES | COOKING TIME: 30 MINUTES | SERVES: 4-6

LA HOGUE FARM SHOP AND CAFÉ

· ·

BY CHRIS REEKS

"I believe farming is either in you or not, and believe me you have to have a weird, almost sadistic, passion for it, as the challenges are huge and often the financial rewards are low."

18 years ago myself and my wife Joanna gave up our professional careers, sold the house and ploughed everything into converting two redundant piggeries into a farm shop and delicatessen on Jo's family farm in Suffolk. We're both children of farmers so had that passion for farming and food production already, and wanted to offer high quality produce from local suppliers and our own farm.

Today, La Hogue Farm Shop and Café is a multi-award-winning business, employing over 45 local staff, and supporting over 100 local and regional farmers and producers. There are full time butchers in the farm shop who prepare our home-grown lamb, traditional breed beef, local free-range pork and chicken, 15 varieties of homemade sausages and local game when it's in season. The large café serves cooked breakfasts (including homemade sausages from the butchers, of course!) and lunches, plus a selection of the most sumptuous desserts, all made on site.

Ten years ago, I got the opportunity to take the grazing rights on the historic Euston Estate which is privately owned by the Duke and Duchess of Grafton, comprising pasture, greening and environmentally grown cover crops. I run a small lambing flock and produce extensively grazed (1 sheep per acre!) free-range lamb for the farm shop and café. Although I hadn't been actively farming since moving from my parents' family farm, I knew I had to take that opportunity. I believe farming is either in you or not, and believe me you have to have a weird, almost sadistic, passion for it, as the challenges are huge and often the financial rewards are low.

Despite the challenges, we've forged ahead, gradually expanding as finances allowed, and run up to 2500 sheep at Euston during peak times. The estate also has its own herd of traditional Red Poll cattle (a breed originating from Suffolk) and I buy many of the extensively reared males for the Farm Shop butchery. We also have our own small herd of Pedigree Highland Cattle, based at La Hogue, which shop and café customers delight in seeing while visiting.

The old cliché that 'farming is a way of life' is so accurate – most farmers wouldn't do it simply for financial reward, with long hours in often challenging weather conditions and the all too frequent heartbreak of losing stock – but for me it is a strange form of escapism…and I wouldn't have it any other way.

SLOW COOKED PULLED LAMB

Lamb has always been one of my favourite meats and this recipe perfectly displays its versatility. The melt-in-the-mouth shoulder is rich and warming and reminds me a little of crispy Peking duck from your Chinese... In fact, I simply reheat any leftovers on the bone and shred the meat off into pancakes or wraps with spring onion, cucumber and sweet chilli or hoisin sauce! – Chris Reeks

1-1.5kg lamb shoulder, bone in

Splash of olive oil

25g butter

4 large onions, peeled and quartered

1 bulb of garlic, cloves separated and peeled

240ml white wine

240ml chicken or beef stock

4 sprigs of fresh rosemary

3 bay leaves

1 lemon, zested

1 tbsp Dijon or wholegrain mustard

2 anchovies

1 tbsp cumin seeds

Salt and black pepper

3 tsp cornflour, mixed with 60ml water

Take the lamb out of the fridge 1 or 2 hours before cooking so it comes to room temperature. Preheat your oven to 130°c and heat a little oil in a large frying pan over a high heat. Add the lamb shoulder, skin side down, and cook until browned. Turn over and brown the other side then set aside on a plate. Drain the excess fat from the pan.

Reduce the heat to medium-high, add the butter to the same pan and cook the onions for a few minutes until golden. Add the garlic cloves and cook for another few minutes. Add the wine, turn up the heat and let it bubble rapidly for a minute while you scrape up any caramelised juices stuck to the bottom. Add the stock, rosemary, bay leaves and lemon zest. Stir then carefully pour everything into your largest roasting dish.

Place the lamb shoulder into the dish, skin side up. Spread the mustard and anchovies over the top and drizzle with olive oil. Sprinkle with the cumin seeds and season with salt and pepper.

Cover the dish tightly with tin foil and bake in the preheated oven for 5 hours or until the meat is falling off the bone. Baste the lamb a couple of times while it's cooking. Remove the tin foil, turn up the oven to 200°c and cook for another 10 to 15 minutes before serving.

Transfer the lamb to a warmed plate or platter – use a dinner plate instead of tongs, as it will be falling apart and very tender – then cover with the foil. Let it rest for 10 to 15 minutes.

To remove the layer of oil on top of the pan juices, gently lay 6 or 7 paper towels on the surface without pressing down. Wait a few minutes for them to soak through, then discard. Pour the remaining pan juices through a sieve into a clean saucepan. Add the cornflour mixture and boil until the liquid has reduced to a nice pouring sauce while the lamb rests. Taste and season as required.

To serve

Pull the lamb into nice big chunks. Serve on mashed potatoes with seasonal vegetables, pour your gravy over the top and scatter with a few fresh herbs for garnish. Leftover lamb can be used to make a great salad or sandwich for lunch the next day.

PREPARATION TIME: 20 MINUTES | COOKING TIME: 5 HOURS 30 MINUTES | SERVES: 6

MOSS VALLEY FINE MEATS

· ·

BY STEPHEN AND KAREN THOMPSON

"As a farmer, you tend to work for the next generation, so we won't see the return on some of what we do, but it's about trying to leave things better than they were."

We produce pork, bacon, ham and sausages in our own butchery from pigs bred and reared on our farm in the beautiful Moss Valley close to the Sheffield-Derbyshire border. The family has lived and farmed here for a hundred years; I'm the fourth generation. We've had pigs on the farm for the last 60 years and been breeding for the last 40 while slowly but surely building our unit up to its current size and then refurbishing everything.

It started really when we got fed up with being ripped off by supermarkets, so we raised and sold just one pig to family members. The feedback was so good we thought we had to try something; Karen went on a few butchery courses but soon realised that others could do the job a lot quicker! She now looks after the animals and I talk to chefs, which we're both happy with. We do 15 pigs in a week with three butchers, which might not sound a lot but it began with one pig every three weeks.

We try to offer a large range of pork produce from our specially selected sows, the majority of which are Large White-Landrace cross breeds. We also use Durocs which give the meat its marbling, making it really tender. The consistency in our farming methods means that you can pretty much guarantee the quality, and the restaurants, cafés and delis using our produce throughout the region are testament to that, especially Street Food Chef, who have grown up with us as a business, and True North who have always been very supportive.

We've always gone down the local route and are the only producer in the world to carry the Made In Sheffield mark; the prestige of that gets us into places, but the quality keeps us there. We have one of the lowest antibiotic uses of any producer in the country, and our cycle of growing feed, raising the animals, using their waste to fertilise more feed creates a healthy system. Sustainability has long been integral to our farm; the farmhouses have been heated by straw burners for decades, and we also have two wind turbines and a borehole for the water supply. As a farmer, you tend to work for the next generation, so we won't see the return on some of what we do, but it's about trying to leave things better than they were.

PORK WITH SWEET POTATO PURÉE AND HARISSA

· ·

Succulent Moss Valley pork belly and fillet are used in this beautiful dish. The crispy pork belly and tender pork fillet sit side by side with flavours from Spain and North Africa.

For the pork

600g Moss Valley pork fillet

8 slices of Parma ham

600g Moss Valley belly pork

1 lemon

Coarse sea salt

For the sweet potato purée

250g sweet potato, peeled and diced

25g butter

Hot sweet smoked paprika

For the harissa

2 tsp ground cumin

20g fresh red chilli, chopped

40g piquillo peppers

3 cloves of garlic

Small bunch of coriander

1 lemon, juiced

30ml olive oil

½ tsp salt

For the green beans and piquillo peppers

150g green beans

50g piquillo peppers

1 tsp cumin seeds

For the pork

Wrap the pork fillet in the Parma ham, roll tightly in cling film to create a cylinder and leave to rest in the fridge while you make the rest of the dish. Cut the lemon in half and rub it on the skin of the belly pork. Sprinkle with the coarse sea salt and leave to rest for 15 minutes.

Preheat the oven to 180°c. Cook the belly pork in the oven for 40 minutes, then turn the oven down to 160°c for the next 40 minutes. Finally, turn the oven down to 140°c for another 40 minutes. When cooked, cut the pork belly into portions. Turn the oven back up to 180°c ready for the pork fillet.

For the sweet potato purée

Boil the sweet potato until soft, then drain and blend with the butter, a pinch of paprika and salt until smooth.

For the harissa

Blend all the ingredients together until well combined. Set aside.

For the green beans and piquillo peppers

Boil the green beans in a pan of water until al dente. Fry the piquillo peppers and cumin seeds together until softened, then add the green beans to the pan and season to taste.

To finish and serve

Pan-fry the pork fillet to sear on all sides, then cook in the preheated oven for about 7 minutes. The centre will be a little pink, but cook for longer if required. Leave to rest for around 5 minutes before carving, then serve the slices of fillet with portions of pork belly, spoonfuls of sweet potato purée and some green beans with peppers, drizzled with harissa.

PEARSON FARM

BY HEATHER PEARSON

"I love that my children are growing up learning where their food comes from. I am proud to be part of a farming business that I believe in."

Becoming a farmer's wife was never something that I envisioned for my life. I'm originally from Canada and my plan had been to combine my passion for travel with work in countries where I could spend as much time in the sun and on the beach as possible. Tom and I met while studying in London and spent the next four years working in Haiti and Sierra Leone, but after we got married in 2014, we moved back to the UK with the plan to start a family and start farming.

Tom's family have been farming for over 300 years and we were honoured to join this tradition on his family farm in Cambridgeshire. During harvest, our son and daughter love watching the tractors. We love spending time outside as a family and Sundays often involve going for walks on the farm to check the crops or picking apples in the garden. I love that my children are growing up learning where their food comes from. I am proud to be part of a farming business that I believe in.

Tom and I share a passion for farming practices and diversification projects that leave a positive environmental and community impact, such as replacing artificial fertilisers with as much organic manure as we can get our hands on, practising regenerative agriculture with no-till or cover crops, providing seasonal cropping and wildlife information signs along our 10km of footpaths, bridleways and permissive paths.

We are already seeing improved soil health and analyse our harvested grains to learn how our plants have grown, and ultimately provide more nutritional food. We currently grow oats, wheat, malting barley, soya, oilseed rape and field beans but are always open to trying new crops. The farm works closely with new agricultural technologies and practices, including robotics and artificial intelligence, and is part of environmental schemes, including a tree planting programme. We have a goal to be net zero carbon farming by 2030.

Being within three miles of six primary schools and a secondary school, we are well placed to open the farm up to school visits and contribute to building positive links between farming and the public. We're always excited to share how the farm works and other projects in the pipeline include using our previous skills in medicine, occupational therapy and public heath to provide wellness opportunities for people through nature and conservation projects on the farm.

MANOR FARM YARD

NANNA'S APPLE CRISP

I wanted to share a dish that was from my Canadian roots but full of British ingredients. We produce oats on our arable farm in Cambridgeshire and grow apples in our garden, so I knew this would be the perfect recipe. Both my British and Canadian families love this and I hope your families do too. – Heather Pearson

For the filling

720g apples (about 6 or 7 large apples)

½ tsp ground cinnamon

125ml water

1 tsp lemon juice

1 tsp lemon zest

For the topping

120g flour

¼ tsp salt

200g brown sugar

45g rolled oats

115g butter

For the filling

Peel and slice the apples, layering them into a 23cm ovenproof dish or casserole dish.

Mix the cinnamon with the water, lemon juice and lemon zest then sprinkle this mixture over the apples.

For the topping

In large bowl, mix the dry ingredients together and cut in the butter. For an extra treat, you could double the topping measurements to add even more crunchy sweetness to this recipe.

Lightly scatter the topping over the apples, without pressing it down, then bake uncovered at 180°c for 45 minutes, then leave it to cool for 10 to 15 minutes.

To serve

Top with a scoop of vanilla ice cream and enjoy warm.

P.X. FARMS

BY JAMES PECK

"As farmers, I think we often do ourselves down, and from my perspective, the main issue is a lack of good marketing. We've got to make it exciting again."

The Peck family business began in 1950 on Scotland Farm and has existed amidst expansions and diversification on that site ever since. I branched out by establishing P.X. Farms in 2003 because I wanted to push forward in the industry. The increasing costs and changing models – where families are no longer expected to take up the mantle – have made farming substantially more difficult since those earlier times, so we've gone down the route of scaling up and using innovative methods to reduce environmental impact and improve yields.

We grow a wide range of crops including wheat destined for bread, malting barley for the lager industry, winter barley for livestock feed, peas, beans and nearly 60,000 tons of sugar beet per year. We also produce honey – not commercially, it all came about because my father-in-law began beekeeping as a hobby – to facilitate the pollination of our mustard crops.

It's a completely different industry to the one I started working in during the 1990s, with a level of sophistication that's far beyond what's often portrayed in the media. For example, we're down to 2cm accuracy when spraying or seeding our crops, and those machines require a host of skills from our workers, without solely relying on physical strength anymore. I employ over 40 members of staff, and we house them with their families because I want people to enjoy working on the farms.

As farmers, I think we often do ourselves down, and from my perspective, the main issue is a lack of good marketing. We've got to make it exciting again; I was fortunate enough to be awarded the Nuffield Farming Scholarship which enabled me to learn about the future of arable farming and bring new ideas back to the UK from countries all over the world. I give talks about modernising farming and go into schools around the country, educating young people about the opportunities in our industry because I want farming to do well and thrive again. I've chaired Cambridgeshire and Bedfordshire CLA, currently chair Henman Brooks Committee, and been part of the Worshipful Company of Farmers all to this end.

I live at Scotland Farm with my wife Fiona, our two daughters, Matilda and Emilia, and family members. I developed a passion for farming at an early age growing up on the family estate and am proud to have grown the business with a clear vision and plenty of enthusiasm.

APPLE, PEAR AND GINGER FLAPJACK

· ·

We have the inevitable fruit trees, of mostly mysterious varieties, dotted around the farm. It's a joy to make delicious compotes in the autumn and to squirrel away bags of it in the freezer, ready for winter suppers, like this humble flapjack zinged up with apple, pear and ginger filling.

250g apple and pear compote

1-2 balls of stem ginger, finely chopped

350g rolled porridge oats (or 150g whole rolled oats, 150g rolled porridge oats and 50g spelt porridge flakes for texture)

¾ tsp ground cinnamon

50g blanched hazelnuts, roughly chopped (or almonds)

¼ tsp fine salt

225g unsalted butter

80g golden syrup

20g stem ginger syrup (from the jar)

100g caster sugar

When making your compote, sit the cooked mixture in a stainless steel sieve over a bowl for a short while to allow the surplus syrup to drain off, otherwise the flapjack may be too sticky on the bottom. Just mash it up a bit if there are lumps of fruit. You could use any compote that takes your fancy; I used a greengage compote that was lurking in the freezer and the flapjack looked wonderful. I often mix apple and pear, mainly to use up the hard pears and to add a bit of texture to the apple. I sweeten the fruit with our farm honey as well as sugar; I don't like the compote to be overly sweet and it's best that way for this recipe, as the flapjack mixture is quite sweet in itself. Lastly, stir the stem ginger into the compote and set aside while you make the flapjack mixture.

Preheat your oven to 200°c or 180°c fan. Lightly grease a 20cm square tin and line it with baking parchment. Mix together the oats, cinnamon, nuts and salt in a mixing bowl until evenly distributed.

In a heavy-based pan, melt the butter and syrups over a low, gentle heat until the butter has melted. Add the caster sugar and stir with a wooden spoon. The sugar should be well mixed but still grainy.

Pour this syrupy mixture into the oat mixture and stir until well combined. Press just over half the flapjack mixture into the prepared baking tin, so that there is a good even coverage. Press it down really firmly with the back of a large spoon. Layer the compote evenly on top, keeping it fractionally away from the edges to prevent the juice seeping out and burning. Scatter the remaining flapjack mixture on top and spread it out to ensure an even layer, remembering to press it down firmly or the flapjack will just fall apart.

Bake in the centre of the preheated oven for 25 to 30 minutes until golden brown, covering the top with a piece of baking parchment after 15 minutes to prevent burning. I also turn the tin at this point for even browning.

Leave the flapjack to cool completely in the tin, gently cutting with a sharp knife while still warm. Store in an airtight container in the fridge for up to 3 days. Best eaten at room temperature.

PREPARATION TIME: 20 MINUTES | COOKING TIME: 30 MINUTES | MAKES: 12

ROOTED IN HULL

BY ADRIAN FISHER

"We operate an inclusive approach, although because we are passionate about provenance our priority is locally grown and produced food. When we need to buy in, we insist on knowing how it was grown, the distance it has travelled, and how it was reared."

I have spent much of my life in farming, mostly on a 120 acre mixed farm with pigs and sheep, and a period of share farming and contracting, including the design and implementation of forestry woodland schemes. I experienced some of the best years one could in farming, but eventually had to concede to economy of scale and lack of cash to invest.

However, the passion for farming was still there and, after a brief time working on a community project in Hull, an opportunity arose. A colleague and I worked on the concept of an urban farm in the centre of Hull, aiming to educate and enthuse individuals and groups to 'connect to good basic food' and counteract the growth of food banks as well as the ignorance around growing and eating.

Rooted in Hull is a 'meanwhile use' installation, which means it has to be completely portable. Working in partnership with Hull College, and approximately 30 businesses, we have established the use of 20ft shipping containers, plus 50 raised beds for the growing of vegetables and salad. We now have five containers – an office, store, shop, kitchen and bakery – as well as two polytunnels. Environmental concerns are creating another stream of interest which we are strongly pursuing; we operate off grid as much as we can, with solar panels, reed beds for the kitchen, and by harvesting water from the Royal Mail building which is next door.

People and groups can now visit and see the environmental and food growing systems actually working. The partnerships we have with local businesses are proving invaluable and, as part of our ethos as an innovative organisation, we are looking at various new projects to install. These include a composting toilet which can use urine to generate electricity, growing micro greens with LED lighting, and an electric charging point, powered by solar panels, for cycles.

We operate an inclusive approach, although because we are passionate about provenance our priority is locally grown and produced food. When we need to buy in, we insist on knowing how it was grown, the distance it has travelled, and how it was reared. We promote UK farmers and growers and pass on knowledge about the rural environment, but would love to have more support in future. We need to get the discussion going as many in the city are desperate to hear direct from the farmers.

FRY BREAD

· ·

We have gone for simple 'fry bread' which we use as a demonstration of what can be done without using an oven. It's still just as tasty and fresh as bread baked in the usual way. – Adrian Fisher

2 tbsp sugar

2 tsp dried yeast

1.1 litres warm water

455g strong white flour

455g ordinary plain flour

2 tsp salt

2 tbsp olive oil, plus extra for frying

Mix together the sugar, yeast and water in a jug. Don't stir the mixture; just leave it for 5 minutes or so until the yeast starts to froth.

Meanwhile, mix the flours and salt together in a very large bowl. Whisk the frothy yeast mixture, make a well in the flour and pour the liquid in along with the oil. Start to combine everything with a wooden spoon, then use your hands to bring the dough together, adding a little more water if necessary. Turn the dough out onto a floured surface and knead for about 10 minutes until smooth and elastic in texture.

Lightly oil the bowl and place the dough back into it, then rub oil over the surface of the dough. Cover the bowl with cling film and leave to prove until the dough has doubled in size. This can take a couple of hours in a warm place. Alternatively, this can be made the night before you intend to cook it, covered and left in a cool place overnight: great if you want to make this part of a breakfast dish!

Pour some olive oil into a frying pan on a moderate to high heat. Tear off small chunks of dough, shape them into patties (or however you prefer – our kids have made snail and sausage shapes) and place these into the pan. Fry the bread for about 4 to 5 minutes on each side.

When cooked, split and fill the fry bread as required. Butter and homemade jam is delicious, as is butter and icing sugar if you have a sweet tooth. We've made fry bread when camping and filled it with fried bacon which makes a filling and nutritious start to an activity-filled day.

PREPARATION TIME: 20 MINUTES, PLUS 2 HOURS PROVING | COOKING TIME: 20-30 MINUTES | SERVES: 4

SAXBY'S CIDER

BY PHIL SAXBY

"We had a small field which I thought would be good for an orchard in order to supply this chap with apples... But I had a change of heart and decided to plant trees for cider making."

I was an arable farmer, and I ran the 900 acre family farm for 16 years. Like many farmers we had a number of small diversifications such as barn lets and liveries. But it was in 2012 that the 'Sliding Doors' moment happened for me, when I was sent a circular letter that was asking farmers if they grew apples, as a producer nearby was making apple juice and wanted to buy local fruit. We had a small field away from the rest of the farm which I thought would be good for an orchard and so I began to plan the trees I was going to buy in order to supply this chap with apples. But before I bought the trees, I had a change of heart and decided to plant trees for cider making.

At the time I had no major aspirations and was only looking to have a bit of fun. We planted 1000 trees and by 2013 we had our first apple crop. Our first cider making process was long and difficult; it took six of us four weeks to crush and ferment 600 litres of apple juice to turn into cider. However, the results were successful and it smelled and tasted good. We drank a lot ourselves and sold some to local shops and pubs: Saxby's Cider was born. Since then we have continued to grow; we have planted more orchards and now use shiny new stainless steel kit which makes the process so much easier. We can now press in an hour what it took us four weeks to do in year one!

As we are based in Northamptonshire (not traditional cider making country) we use a blend of bittersweet cider apples from the West Country such as Dabinett, Yarlington Mill and Michelin, and dessert apples, mainly Jonagold, Bramley and Gala. This blend is a perfect balance of crisp acidity and tannins; it has stayed the same since we started and provides a true craft cider that has an easy drinking medium dry flavour for all to enjoy. We have now expanded into fruit flavours, liqueurs, vinegar and even apple juice! We have also won various national and international awards for our drinks: quite a journey all from a chance letter.

And finally…why the pig logo? Well, apart from the fact they go very well with apple sauce, it's because our family used to have a business selling pork pies and sausages which ran for 100 years and the pig is a memento of those days. I hope you enjoy our recipe, and please come and say hello in our shop if you are passing.

LOW & SLOW ROASTED PORK

· ·

This recipe is a Saxby family favourite. Not only is it delicious but it can provide great leftovers for pulled pork rolls another day. A big advantage to the low and slow cooking time is you can leave it cooking all day (or overnight) while getting on with other things.

4 medium carrots, each cut into 3 pieces

3 onions, peeled and quartered

2 apples, quartered

2 whole bulbs of garlic

1 bunch of fresh thyme

6kg pork shoulder on the bone, with scored skin (from your local butcher)

Olive oil

Salt and pepper

500ml Saxby's Original Cider

500ml chicken stock

Preheat your oven to 220°c. Put the roughly chopped carrots, onions, apples, bulbs of garlic and thyme sprigs into a large roasting tray.

Pat the pork shoulder all over with olive oil and sit it on top of the vegetables. Now massage the salt and pepper into the skin of the pork.

Put the tray on a low shelf in your preheated oven to cook for 30 minutes or until it's beginning to colour, then turn your oven down to 120°c and leave the pork for 9 hours or until you can pull the meat apart easily with a fork.

At this stage, tip the cider into the roasting tray and let it cook for another hour. Take the pork out of the oven and let it rest for half an hour before transferring it to a large board. Cover the meat with foil and let it rest.

Remove the vegetables and add the chicken stock to the roasting tray. Put it on the heat, and reduce until you have a lovely gravy. Strain before serving.

Serve with potatoes and green vegetables of your choice and more Saxby's Cider. Cheers!

PREPARATION TIME: 15 MINUTES | COOKING TIME: 10 HOURS | SERVES: 12 (EASILY)

SHARPHAM CHEESE

BY GREG PARSONS

"We see consumers getting more discerning and curious about where their food comes from and our vision is to continue to make high quality cheese with the best possible ingredients, using skills that have been honed for over 40 years."

Nestled in the beautiful valley overlooking the River Dart in South Devon, Sharpham is the realisation of Maurice and Ruth Ash's vision, which began with the slump in milk prices during the 1970s, prompting Maurice to find a way to make his favourite cheese. He moved his herd of Jersey cows from Essex to Devon by train, employed Isa Caroll to set up the dairy in the old stables and started to perfect the making of Sharpham Brie.

The next chapter of the Sharpham story began with family member Mark overseeing the newly-planted vineyards and his partner Debbie heading up the cheesemaking team. They introduced new cheeses such as Elmhirst Triple Cream and Sharpham Rustic (plus its garlic and chive counterpart which was developed after the cows chowed down on wild garlic one day!). Due to growing demand, Mark and Debbie decided to expand with a purpose-built dairy in 2003 and began using ewe's and goat's milk to create more new products.

In 2018, wanting to step back after more than 35 years, Mark and Debbie sought a new partner with the same passion for artisan cheese making and a strong sense of why Devon is such a special place to produce. I was born and bred here and had worked in the dairy industry for the past 20 years, so we hit it off straight away and I invested in Sharpham in 2019, with the condition that Mark and Debbie stay around for a while (albeit with a few more holidays in the calendar).

Today we make 60 to 70 tons of cheese per year, using milk mainly from our own herd of Jersey cows, along with goat's and sheep's milk from a few neighbours. We exist because of our very loyal and long-term customers, many of whom have been buying from us for well over 30 years, mostly supplying delis and restaurants across the West Country, but there's a growing market in London and even a couple of customers sending cheese overseas, as far as California and Australia.

Looking ahead, we see consumers getting more discerning and curious about where their food comes from and our vision is to continue to make high quality cheese with the best possible ingredients, using skills that have been honed for over 40 years here at Sharpham.

SHARPHAM WASHBOURNE, LEEK & WILD GARLIC TART

· ·

Wild garlic is a delicious perennial that grows in abundance on the Sharpham estate. It partners perfectly with cheese, so they find themselves paired together in many different dishes at The Cellar Door, our onsite restaurant. It is available from late winter through to the end of spring. – Daniel Teage and Charlie Ramsdale

For the pastry

170g plain flour, plus a little extra for dusting

110g unsalted butter

60g Sharpham Washbourne Cheese

¼ tsp cayenne pepper

½ tsp salt

1 egg yolk

For the filling

1 large leek, finely shredded

60g unsalted butter

40g wild garlic

40g spinach

1 free-range egg, plus 2 yolks

90ml double cream

80g Sharpham Washbourne cheese

For the topping

1 large leek

30g unsalted butter

250ml chicken stock

150g Sharpham Washbourne Cheese

For the wild garlic oil

40g wild garlic

60ml rapeseed oil

To serve

12 baby leeks

Few sprigs of chervil

Few small wild garlic leaves

For the pastry

Pulse all the ingredients except the egg yolk together in a food processor with a tablespoon of iced water until the pastry just comes together. Wrap in cling film and chill in the fridge while you make the filling.

Roll the pastry out to 3mm thickness, cut out four circles and place them into a non-stick 10cm tart case. Prick the bases with a fork, then place a circle of greaseproof paper on top and fill with baking beans. Blind bake at 160°c for 15 minutes, then remove the baking beans and bake for a further 5 minutes until golden. Glaze the inside of the tart cases with egg yolk, then bake for 1 minute.

For the filling

Put the leek in a pan over a low heat with the butter and cook slowly until tender. Allow to cool. Blanch the wild garlic in boiling water for 15 seconds, then place in cold water to cool. Drain, then blend with the spinach and 20ml of water until smooth, then blend in the egg, yolks and cream. Season with salt and black pepper.

Divide the cooked leeks between the tarts, then crumble 20g of cheese into each. Fill the tarts to the top with the wild garlic and spinach mixture. Bake at 150°c until the tops are set and they no longer wobble: around 25 to 30 minutes.

For the topping

Slice the leek into 1cm rounds. Place in a single layer in a pan with the butter and stock, and gently simmer until tender. Allow to cool. On a metal tray, arrange the poached leeks into four rounds, interspersed with 1cm lumps of cheese. Colour the top with a blowtorch, or under a very hot grill, then transfer onto your tarts.

For the wild garlic oil

Blanch the garlic in boiling water for 15 seconds, refresh in cold water, then squeeze out as much water as possible. Blend with the oil and a pinch of salt on high speed for 3 minutes, then strain through muslin to make a clear oil.

To serve

Grate any remaining cheese evenly into a non-stick frying pan. Cook over a low heat until the cheese turns golden brown. Remove from the pan and allow to cool, then break into shards. Chargrill the baby leeks for 1 or 2 minutes each side. Garnish the tarts with chervil, wild garlic leaves and cheese shards, arrange the baby leeks on the side, drizzle with wild garlic oil and serve.

SILVERTON VINEYARD

···

BY IVAN JORDAN

"We cherished sunny afternoons in our Exeter allotment...bringing home food that could not be bought: sweetcorn and asparagus barely minutes old, spicy exotic salad leaves, courgette flowers, grapes from our vines. So we took our love of growing things to a new level, on our terms, on our own land."

Townies. That's what we are. An architect and a DJ, farming. Cluelessly sticking the car in ditches, planting saplings that get eaten, putting up polytunnels that get blown down, and making countless other mistakes. But, ten years in, we have two innovative, profitable businesses on our land, producing the most sustainable sparkling wine in the world, in the heart of beautiful Devon.

Ten years ago we had a moment in life to make a move. We cherished sunny afternoons in our Exeter allotment; gorging on plums from the tree we planted, dipping toes in our little pond, hoeing the shallots, and bringing home food that could not be bought: sweetcorn and asparagus barely minutes old, spicy exotic salad leaves, courgette flowers, grapes from our vines.

But we didn't enjoy the oppressive conservatism of allotment politics, especially the wholescale spraying of glyphosate by our neighbours, who in turn did not enjoy the presence of our children. So we took our love of growing things to a new level, on our terms, on our own land.

We wanted to establish a business on the land that would outlast us, a new family farm. English wine was gaining credibility, and research revealed eight local vineyards, all doing well. We re-mortgaged the house, and went all in on 17 acres of south-facing Devon farmland, planting 2000 vines. This is Silverton Vineyard. The timescale and investment of winemaking was potentially ruinous, so a second cash-generating initiative was started too: Greens of Devon is our rural micro-business, growing fresh edible flowers and herbs naturally and seasonally. When you see an edible flower on a cake on TV, it probably came from us.

The wine we have developed is unique. As the vines we planted grew, we researched, experimented, got it wrong, and got it right. We ignored convention, refused to spray our vines with anything, lost some harvests and were swamped by others. We built a solar-powered winery, off-grid, right by the vines. From grape to bottle, we created a new process that captures in wine the things we love most about growing: the sweet, crisp, acidic, juicy flavours of freshness.

THE SILVER BULLET

· ·

Our recipe is a cocktail, like Silverton Vineyard itself. It is town and country, tradition and innovation, a beautiful fusion of flavours, fragrances and colours, in ebullient style.
– Ivan Jordan

25ml vodka

Bottle of chilled Silverton wine

1 egg white, whipped to a froth, with

1 tsp sugar

Dash of grenadine

1 jelly bean

1 orange blossom

1 lime, zested

Pour the vodka into a champagne flute and top up with the wine, leaving half an inch to the rim. Whip the egg white to a froth with the sugar, then gently pour it into the glass to create a fluffy meringue-ish top. Pour the dash of grenadine gently into the centre, then drop the jelly bean into the glass from six inches above, so it punctures the top and falls to the bottom, taking a stream of red grenadine with it. Place an edible flower over the hole, and sprinkle lime zest on top. Enjoy!

PREPARATION TIME: 5 MINUTES | SERVES: 1

SOUTH DEVON CHILLI FARM

BY HEATHER & STEVE WATERS, MARTIN & KAZ PHILLIPS

"We started growing chillies as a hobby in our back garden greenhouses when we moved to rural Devon, and soon realised that they were easy to grow and completely addictive."

Here on our 10 acre farm in sunny South Devon, we are passionate about growing, cooking, eating and talking about chillies. We love all the subtle flavours they offer as well as, of course, the heat! We started growing chillies as a hobby in our back garden greenhouses when we moved to rural Devon, and soon realised that they were easy to grow and completely addictive.

An opportunity arose to rent a polytunnel and we decided to see how many different varieties we could grow. Suddenly, we had lots and didn't know what to do with them all. Fortunately, farmers' markets had started to become popular and so we took our amazing crop of fresh chillies to the markets and some local shows. We got an immediate positive response from the public and realised there was a widespread fascination with chillies. As we hadn't sold all our fresh chillies, we then headed to our kitchens to experiment with different recipes for preserving them.

Our very first product was the Hot Apple Chilli Jelly which we made with local orchards' apples, simply boiled up with sugar and a little chilli, naturally set thanks to the pectin in the apples. We went on to create other chilli preserves using either vinegar or sugar, and still stick to our original method of natural preserving today, as well as using drying and smoking techniques. All our products are made in small batches, retaining their lovely home-cooked flavour.

In 2003, we gave up our day jobs to grow chillies and cook up new products full time, becoming a limited company and creating a website to sell our chilli products across the country. In 2005, we were lucky enough to have a fellow farmer offer to sell us 10 acres of precious farmland. On our new site, we built a large barn to house a production kitchen and a storage facility for the huge number of jars and bottles we were starting to get through each month, plus six polytunnels.

During the growing season today, you can buy plants and fresh chillies and wander through our Show Tunnel where around 200 varieties of chilli plants are on display. In 2011, there were enough funds to add our fabulous farm shop and café; you can now stop for a drink or lunch and enjoy the views, then 'try before you buy' with our chilli sauces, chilli preserves and chilli chocolates.

CHILLI CHOCOLATE BROWNIES

· ·

These brownies are really popular in our on-site café, particularly served with clotted cream! We use our 60% cocoa Orange Chilli Chocolate, but they would be equally good with our original chilli chocolate which gives your classic brownie a delightfully different twist, with just a touch of spice.

360g unsalted butter, melted

150g cocoa powder

600g caster sugar

Few drops of vanilla essence

200g plain flour

1 ½ tsp baking powder

8 eggs, lightly beaten

220g South Devon Chilli Farm Orange Chilli Chocolate, broken into pieces (or 160g chilli chocolate and 60g plain chocolate)

Preheat the oven to 160°c. Line a 24 by 32cm (6cm deep) baking tin with baking parchment.

Mix the melted butter, cocoa, sugar and vanilla in a food processor until just mixed. With the machine running slowly, add the flour, baking powder and eggs until combined.

Turn off the mixer and fold in the orange chilli chocolate pieces. Pour the brownie batter into the lined tin and bake in the preheated oven for 30 to 40 minutes or until it's just setting and the surface is beginning to crack.

Allow to cool in the tin and then cut into portions.

PREPARATION TIME: 10 MINUTES | COOKING TIME: 30-40 MINUTES | SERVES: 12

SOUTH FARM

BY JANE PRICE

"To be custodians of our beautiful venue is a true privilege and one that every single member of our team takes very seriously."

We are blessed with a stunning location in a lovely corner of England. We care deeply about the environment and looking after our little part of the world is a big priority for us. Our farm spans over 20 acres and is a tapestry of orchards, vegetable fields, grazing paddocks, herb beds and protected cropping areas. When the site was bought by the Paxman family in 1974 South Farm was a blank canvas of arable fields. Since then a constantly evolving planting and landscaping programme has created beautiful gardens alongside over 1000 indigenous hardwood trees, heritage orchards and kilometres of hedgerow providing diverse wildlife habitats.

We are not only a working farm, we are also an award-winning wedding venue with a country farmhouse, converted barns and garden summerhouse. Our ethos is to give couples the very best wedding day possible in a beautiful setting, with impeccable service in a friendly and relaxed manner. Food is hugely important to us. All our weddings are catered in-house by our team of talented chefs who create seasonal menus starring home-grown produce. We offer a diverse range of menus, including full vegan and vegetarian menus. Surplus produce goes to a food sharing organisation who distribute food within our local community.

We farm using solely organic principles and only externally source what we really have to. We grow a large percentage of the fruit, vegetables and herbs used by our chefs in our smallholding. 140 free-range chickens give us all the eggs needed in our kitchens and we have a free-range herd of Kune Kune and Saddleback pigs so our home-reared pork is fully traceable. Other rare breeds include white peacocks and runner ducks, alongside our sheep and lambs. We also produce juices, jams, preserves and pickles using produce from our small holding and Heritage Orchard. Our over-winter storage for crops such as squash, garlic and onions means they can be used in our menus throughout the seasons.

To be custodians of our beautiful venue is a true privilege and one that every single member of our team takes very seriously. We are committed to being green with a large number of ongoing eco-friendly initiatives. We constantly strive to take steps to reduce the impact that our activities and actions have on the environment and we were proud winners of the Outstanding Rural Diversification Project at The Rural Business Awards in 2018.

HOME-GROWN HERITAGE TOMATO SALAD

In the summer months, our many varieties of tomato plant burst with colourful fruit. Some of the most interesting tomatoes we grow are Indigo Beauty, Golden Sunrise, Red and Green Zebra and Giagantomo. Using a mix of varieties and sizes will enhance the visual impact and deliciousness of this salad.

100ml aged Aceto Balsamico de Modena vinegar (or any other good quality balsamic vinegar)

2g agar-agar (a vegetarian alternative to gelatine)

1 or 2 of each tomato variety you have (use as many colours, sizes and textures as available)

20g smoked Maldon sea salt

20 basil leaves

50ml aged Aceto Balsamico De Modena glaze

250g burrata (or buffalo mozzarella)

5g basil cress (or very young basil)

5g shiso cress (optional)

100ml good quality extra-virgin olive oil

20ml basil oil

For the balsamic jelly cubes

Bring the balsamic vinegar to the boil, then stir in the agar-agar using a whisk. Make sure it has all been dissolved. Line a small tray with cling film and pour the balsamic mix into the tray. Leave the jelly to set in the fridge for at least 1 hour. This can be done a day in advance. Once set, tip the contents of the tray onto a chopping board and dice the jelly into 1cm cubes.

To prepare the tomatoes

Cut each tomato into different shapes, letting their shape guide you. Don't go for the same size pieces. Some tomatoes naturally lend themselves to being cut into large chunks, others could be sliced, and some, for example baby plum tomatoes, could be left whole or simply halved. The aim is to have a variety of shapes, sizes, colours and textures. Once you are happy with the mixture of tomatoes, season them with the smoked Maldon sea salt. Tear the basil leaves into pieces using your fingers and add them to the tomatoes. Toss them in the bowl to mix everything together, then cover the bowl with cling film and leave to sit on the side for up to 15 minutes. The salt will season the tomatoes and release their wonderful flavour.

To assemble

Place four plates in front of you. Dip a pastry brush into the balsamic glaze and spread some in the centre of each plate. Divide the seasoned tomatoes between the plates, making sure that every serving has a variety of shapes and sizes. Tear the burrata or mozzarella into 12 pieces and divide them between the four plates. Add five or six cubes of balsamic jelly to each plate, but if you love balsamic then feel free to add more! Sprinkle the basil cress and shiso over the top then finish the salad with a drizzle of extra-virgin olive oil and basil oil.

The result will be four stunning plates full of colour and flavour! Our recipe is for a starter, but to make this salad into a main course, follow the steps above but split everything between two large plates instead to serve.

SOUTH FARM

·····································

BY JEMMA PYNE

"Farming to me is the most noble of jobs. I wouldn't want to be anywhere else and I'm eternally grateful that my children will grow up knowing this life."

Growing up, the only experience I had of farms were childhood holidays to a working farm in Crediton which I loved, but I never really thought a farm might feature in my future. I suffer with allergies so a farm is kind of my nemesis! Then I met and married Nick and became a farmer's wife. His family have been farming for many generations and Nick works with his uncle in Budleigh Salterton, a beautiful farm on the south west coast of Devon. They produce wheat, barley, maize, a variety of vegetables, keep a small flock of sheep for lamb, and 600 free-range chickens for eggs.

It turns out that woolly beings don't upset my allergies, which has been the most amazing discovery and allows me to plough all my pent up love of animals into them! I love taking care of the sheep but Nick and I had twins, Bessie and Toby, in 2017 so my time with the animals has dramatically reduced over the last few years. It is the most rewarding job but it also has incredibly difficult times too. Losing livestock never gets less heartbreaking, particularly when you've put a huge amount of blood, sweat and tears into helping them. It is a true labour of love.

Growing crops is a masterpiece of organisation from preparing the land to harvest. There is also land set aside for wildlife and natural plant growth that has to be considered, as caring for the environment in our Area of Outstanding Natural Beauty is very important. Our planter is a contraption pulled slowly along by the tractor. Five people sit in a row in the planter, feeding the seedlings in by hand and the machine puts them into the ground in spaced rows. It's backbreaking work and the bumpy ride can cause motion sickness! At our farm we try not to use chemicals unless absolutely necessary so for the most part weeding is done by hand too.

Farming to me is the most noble of jobs. The work that goes into it is unimaginable and sadly for very little return in monetary terms. My husband wouldn't want to do anything else though, he loves being outside and he loves every day being completely different from the last. Each day brings new learning opportunities and challenges to rise to. I wouldn't want to be anywhere else and I'm eternally grateful that my children will grow up knowing this life.

WINTER VEGETABLE GRATIN

This is a go-to recipe in our household because it uses vegetables we grow and it's versatile. I have been known to add broccoli, cauliflower and even kale. It can be eaten as a side dish or as a vegetarian standalone meal. It's easy to prepare and a delicious comfort food for the cold winter evenings. – Jemma Pyne

500g potatoes, sliced wafer thin

1 large parsnip, sliced wafer thin

1 large beetroot, sliced wafer thin

1 large sweet potato, sliced wafer thin

3 cloves of garlic, thinly sliced

Pinch of salt

1 tbsp chopped fresh rosemary

275ml double cream

150ml full-fat milk

60g Parmesan, grated

Preheat the oven to 180°c and butter a shallow ovenproof dish. Layer some of the potatoes, then parsnip, beetroot, and sweet potato in the dish. At the halfway point, scatter over two of the sliced garlic cloves, a little salt and half the rosemary. Keep making layers until you have used all the vegetables.

Pour the cream and milk into a saucepan then add the rest of the rosemary and garlic, half the Parmesan and a little seasoning. Gently heat for 3 minutes.

Pour the cream mixture over the layered vegetables. Sprinkle over the remaining Parmesan, cover the whole dish with foil and bake for 40 minutes. Remove the foil and bake for a further 15 minutes until golden and bubbly.

If you don't like Parmesan, just replace it with a good quality cheddar, or if you want the gratin to be extra cheesy, sprinkle cheddar on top in addition to the Parmesan.

JW & PA STANLEY & SON

···

BY JOE STANLEY

"Carbon-neutral food is within our grasp, and traditional, predominantly grazed native breeds of livestock like our Longhorns are a key part of that future. In order to succeed, we just need the support of our consumers."

I'm the third generation of my family to produce food from our land on the edge of the beautiful Charnwood Forest in Leicestershire, in partnership with my parents, John and Pat, and alongside my trusty Jack Russell companions Ted and Toby. We are a traditional lowland mixed farm, currently running a herd of prize-winning pedigree Longhorn cattle – the 'Blackbrook' herd, taking its name from the swift-flowing stream which bisects our farm – and growing combinable arable crops such as wheat, barley and oilseeds. We also run sheep on areas of the farm which more closely resemble the uplands of the Peak District than the low river valleys of Leicestershire!

Our livestock and arable enterprises are complementary; straw from our crops is used as bedding for our cattle in the winter, with the resulting muck returning to the fields as precious organic fertiliser which maintains soil health. We are particularly proud of our Longhorns, a local breed originally improved by the great agricultural pioneer Robert Bakewell in the 18th century, and the first recognised pedigree. He developed them to produce a greater quantity of meat to feed the workers of a rapidly industrialising nation, but they also possess very rich milk and their spectacular horns were widely prized for a variety of uses. Today, they provide wondrous, slow-finishing, marbled meat which we are lucky enough to provide friends, family and farm shops with. Thanks to this, we are recent winners of the Country Life 'Meat of the Year' accolade.

We have also exported embryos from our purebred cattle around the world, re-introducing the Longhorn to countries such as Australia, which will not have seen them since colonial times and where they have thrived. As a farmer, I acknowledge that we will need to increase global food production to feed 10 billion people by 2050; I also know that we will have to do this in a more sustainable fashion, with lower impacts on biodiversity and fewer greenhouse gas emissions. I believe that British farmers are already well-placed to lead this change; we operate to some of the highest welfare, environmental and food safety standards in the world, and strive to become a NetZero industry by 2040.

Carbon-neutral food is within our grasp, and traditional, predominantly grazed native breeds of livestock like our Longhorns are a key part of that future: Britain possesses a wealth of genetic diversity. In order to succeed, we just need the support of our consumers in continuing to back British farming.

BLACKBROOK BEEF BOLOGNESE

A great summer dish: the majority of ingredients can be sourced seasonally from UK growers, and a good Bolognese needs top-quality steak mince such as that produced by our native Longhorns. Shop locally and seasonally for the best ingredients! – Joe Stanley

1 large onion

2 large bell peppers

300g closed cup mushrooms

200g cherry tomatoes

30ml UK rapeseed oil

500g beef mince

1 tin (400g) of chopped tomatoes

50g tomato purée

20g garlic paste

2 beef stock cubes

15ml Bovril

5ml Worcestershire sauce

1 tbsp dried oregano

Salt and black pepper, coarsely ground

Small handful of fresh basil

300g linguine

100g British cheese, grated

Chop the onion, peppers, mushrooms and cherry tomatoes. Heat the oil in a wide pan, then add the prepared vegetables except the cherry tomatoes and fry to your preference. Add the mince and fry until browned. Drain off any excess liquid at this point.

Tip the chopped tomatoes into the pan, along with the cherry tomatoes. Reduce to a simmer. Add the tomato purée and garlic paste then stir well. Crumble in the stock cubes and stir to dissolve them. Add the Bovril and Worcestershire sauce (these are optional, for a strong beefy taste!).

Stir in the oregano then season to your preference with salt and pepper. Finally, tear in the basil (keeping a few leaves for garnish) and reduce the heat to a low simmer for 15 minutes. Stir once or twice. Meanwhile, cook the linguine in a separate pan with a dash of rapeseed oil to prevent the pasta sticking. When it's ready, drain the linguine and serve with the Bolognese. Garnish with grated cheese and a few basil leaves.

PREPARATION TIME: 10 MINUTES | COOKING TIME: 30 MINUTES | SERVES: 4

TRACTORS AND TWEED

· ·

BY BETH WITHERS

"My journey from complete novice to farmer co-hand was a steep learning curve, and it still continues. I loved every minute of it: I discovered new terms, learnt how to care for and handle animals, visited the local markets and nearly fainted when I saw my first lamb born."

With two children under two, four dogs, a whole host of chickens, ducks and guineas, a family butchers and the farm to help with, it's fair to say I love being busy!

My husband is the fifth generation of his family at Lowlands Farm. We have 500 ewes, 60 suckler cows and also grow cereals to produce feed and bedding. Me, I wasn't a farmer at all. I was brought up in the countryside but moved to London at 21 and began a corporate life. It was when I moved back to the Midlands that I met the man who is now my husband in the local pub. Our dates consisted of being in the lambing shed and messing about at the farm; with me loving to bake and a hungry farmer in tow, the rest was history. Four years later we married, and now have two boys.

My journey from complete novice to farmer co-hand was a steep learning curve, and it still continues. I loved every minute of it: I discovered new terms, learnt how to care for and handle animals, visited the local markets and nearly fainted when I saw my first lamb born.

All this inspired me to set up a blog called Tractors and Tweed. The tractors are everything 'farm' and the tweed is everything 'home'. I wanted to share my journey with others and let those who didn't have access to the farming world have an insight into farming life. It began with just an Instagram account, but I have now expanded into a blog and YouTube channel to help share our journey in a multitude of ways. The reception has been great and there is nothing more satisfying than to get feedback from those trying out new recipes or just asking questions about the animals.

I would love to take this journey off social media and onto the farm by offering courses and experiences to the general public. Maybe that will be the next step for our farm, but who knows, although who doesn't like to see a newborn lamb?

It's an exciting time for us as a family and I can't wait to see what the sixth generation will bring to our farm. Until then, we will keep sharing our passion and continue to do what we love.

ROCK CAKES

· ·

This is a family favourite in our house and a recipe that has been used for generations. You can mix up the inclusions using whatever you have in your cupboard; I love chocolate chips and cherries. Oh, and they taste best warm, straight from the oven! – Beth Withers

230g self-raising flour

115g margarine

115g caster sugar

115g dried fruit (or your favourite additions)

1 egg, beaten

2 tbsp milk

Sprinkling of sugar, to finish

Sieve the flour into a mixing bowl and then rub in the margarine until the mixture resembles fine breadcrumbs. Stir in the sugar and dried fruit, or whichever additions you are using.

Add the beaten egg and milk to the bowl a little at a time, stirring gently, until you get a sticky consistency. Spoon the mixture onto greased baking trays in ten small splodges. They will spread out when they cook so make sure you leave space between each one. Sprinkle the top of each one with sugar.

Bake the rock cakes at 220°c for 15 minutes until golden brown. Leave to cool slightly before enjoying. Simply serve warm with a pot of tea!

PREPARATION TIME: 10 MINUTES | COOKING TIME: 15 MINUTES | SERVES: 10

THE WIFE BEHIND THE FARMER

BY HANNAH MORGAN

"The journey has not been without its struggles; trying to highlight the woman's role on the farm was hard for a lot of the older generation to get their heads around. On the flip side, I love being part of such a forward-thinking and dynamic industry."

Born and raised in Worcestershire, I have never settled anywhere else. After graduating from Harper Adams University College I returned home where I met Matthew, who is now my husband. We were both members of Worcestershire Young Farmers (different clubs I might add), dated for seven years and then finally got married. We moved into his family farm in 2014; he is a third generation farmer whose family have farmed here for over 95 years.

The farm is 206 acres of mixed arable and pasture land; we have a suckler herd and around 140 head of sheep. Over the years we have embarked on various diversification projects and to date our most ambitious project is a doggy day care facility, which we were awarded a LEADER grant for. Aside from helping out on the farm I am mummy to two outdoors-loving children who are very keen to keep farming in the family; Max is tractor-mad and Nancy has a special way with the animals.

In between the challenges of the farm and motherhood I have pursued my own interests in promoting and supporting other farmer's wives who face similar obstacles. This is how 'The Wife Behind The Farmer' was born. I write about topics surrounding the farm and bringing up a family in the farming environment. I have also been providing support for other farmer's wives who want to start their own businesses around their everyday farm life. By promoting their services and products I am a massive advocate of 'Buy Small, Give Big'. I will always post about anything showcasing British design, a love for the agricultural industry and a passion for our countryside.

From developing my vision and being active on social media, I was lucky enough to be a finalist at The British Farming Awards in the digital innovator category in 2018. This really boosted my confidence and gave what I was doing a real seal of approval. The journey has not been without its struggles; trying to highlight the woman's role on the farm was hard for a lot of the older generation to get their heads around. On the flip side, I love being part of such a forward-thinking and dynamic industry. British agriculture has so many sides to it and we all play our part in some way. I'm sure you'll all agree that behind every strong farmer, there's an even stronger wife or partner.

TIPSY FOOL

· ·

My tipsy fool is a twist on an English classic. As a family we love naughty desserts and this really fits the bill. All the ingredients can be sourced locally (even from your garden) which is something I'm really passionate about. (Why not try swapping the raspberries for a different berry or rhubarb? – Hannah Morgan

100g fresh raspberries

30g caster sugar

3 tbsp Chase Elderflower Liqueur

300ml whipping cream

55g icing sugar

1 or 2 shortbread biscuits, crumbled

Sprigs of fresh mint, to garnish (optional)

Set a few whole raspberries aside for garnish. In a bowl, stir the rest of the raspberries gently with the caster sugar and elderflower liqueur, then let them sit for 10 to 15 minutes.

Whip the cream with the icing sugar until soft peaks form.

Mash the raspberries with a fork until all the liquid and fruit is combined.

Spoon half the fruit into the whipped cream and fold once or twice with a rubber spatula; do not overmix!

Add half of the remaining fruit and fold once or twice. You can either add the rest now, or use the last bit of raspberry purée on top.

Serve the fool spooned into pretty glasses with the crumbled shortbread and sprigs of mint on top, and a shot of the elderflower liqueur on the side if you like! This is best made right before serving.

ROCK AND ROLL FARMING

· ·

BY WILL EVANS

"I'm not sure there's ever been a more exciting time to be in this industry than right now, standing as we are on the verge of a fourth agricultural revolution."

I come from a very long line of farmers. My family have farmed in this area of Wales since at least the early 1700s, and probably further back than that. I suppose you could say that this way of life, and the very land itself, is in my DNA. In recent years we've found artefacts including a Roman coin and a medieval silver brooch in some of our fields, which suggests that food has been produced here for at least two thousand years. It gives me a powerful feeling that I'm part of something important; that I'm just this farm's present custodian, holding it in trust for the next generation.

Agriculture in this country is about many different things. There are world famous landscapes: if you're ever in a plane flying back into the UK, look down at that breathtakingly unique patchwork scene below, hedges and stone walls, mountains and valleys, rivers and lakes, and all worked and shaped by the farmers and people of the land since time immemorial.

It's about ground-breaking innovation and technology; throughout history, some of the most widely adopted and successful advances in farming techniques have come from the UK, and I'm not sure there's ever been a more exciting time to be in this industry than right now, standing as we are on the verge of a fourth agricultural revolution. There's the incredible native breed livestock that farming families have put their heart and soul into breeding over generations, and spend countless hours rearing and caring for, in some of the highest animal welfare systems anywhere in the world.

But more than all of these things, it's about the people: the farmers and their families, and the rural communities in which they live. The ones who are getting up every morning to do the job that they love, because there's nothing else on earth they'd rather be doing.

It's for this reason that I started the Rock & Roll Farming podcast in 2017. I wanted to talk to those involved in the agricultural industry and help to share their stories with the wider world, to highlight the grit, determination, talent, work ethic, drive, and entrepreneurship that goes into producing the high quality and affordable food that we all enjoy in this country. There's nothing like food for bringing people together. Whether it's a meal out with friends, or a family dinner around the kitchen table, I'm extremely proud of the contribution we make to this as Britain's farmers.

PHEASANT BREASTS WITH CARAMELISED APPLE, BACON, AND MUSTARD MASH

....

Between running a busy farm, and bringing up four young daughters, we don't have a lot of time for cooking elaborate meals for the family. But we do try to eat as healthily as we can, and make the most of our natural surroundings: this dish is perfect for that! – Will Evans

45g butter

6 large pheasant breasts

75g smoked bacon lardons

6 shallots, peeled

3 small apples, sliced

3 tbsp whisky (more if it's a Saturday night)

750g floury potatoes, peeled and cubed

2 tbsp fresh parsley

2 tbsp wholegrain mustard

3 tbsp sour cream

300ml good quality chicken stock

Salt and freshly ground pepper

Pour yourself a large glass of wine, put some classic Springsteen on, and preheat the oven to 200°c or 180°c with fan. Chuck all that lovely butter (strictly no margarine allowed) into a non-stick frying pan and place over a high heat, until it's bubbling nicely. Add the pheasant breasts and brown them on all sides, before putting them aside on a warm plate.

Sling the bacon, shallots, and sliced apple into the pan, and fry over a medium heat until it's all browning. Add the whisky, and now for the fun part: flame it! When the alcohol has burnt off, spoon the mixture into a small roasting tin, and arrange the pheasant breasts on top.

Pour yourself another large glass of wine while it cooks in the preheated oven for 25 to 30 minutes, until the meat is just tender and the juices run clear.

Bring a large pan of salted water to the boil and add the potato cubes. Boil until tender, drain, then add the parsley, wholegrain mustard and sour cream. Mash until smooth.

Remove the pheasant, bacon, shallots and apples from the pan. Cover and set aside. Lash the stock into the pan and bring to the boil, scraping up any residue. Season the sauce with salt and pepper.

Serve the pheasant breasts with the caramelised apples, shallots and lardons, the pan juices spooned over, the mash on the side, some purple sprouting broccoli, and preferably another glass of wine. This dish is also good with chicken thighs if you don't have any pheasant handy.

WOODVIEW FARM

BY GEOFF TITMUS

"Our two eldest sons were involved from the start with our youngest son and daughter joining shortly after, so we are very much a family-run business."

We're not a farm so much as a small holding, which has been built up over the years to supply the farm shop that we opened in 2007.

Woodview Farm's roots were as a market garden back in the 70s and 80s, but by the 90s the rise of the supermarket giants forced the closure of many independent greengrocers and market stalls (who were our buyers) which in turn instigated the demise of hundreds of market gardens across the country, ours included.

By the millennium we had established ourselves as a free-range egg producer and had plans to open a farm shop – which were becoming popular – but it wasn't until 2007 that we opened ours, when one of our sons became a qualified butcher. In fact, our two eldest sons were involved from the start with our youngest son and daughter joining shortly after, so we are very much a family-run business.

We source local produce whenever possible and, by taking on more land, have grown the smallholding to around 120 acres. This is predominantly grass for grazing to produce our own lamb and pork. We have flocks of pure Suffolk and Charollais sheep which we cross with North Country mules, and around 20 purebred Large White sows which we breed with Hampshire or Welsh boars. Of course, we must not forget the eggs from our 3000 hens which are extremely popular and always in high demand.

In June 2014 we added a bistro-style café to complement and showcase the produce sold in the shop. Meals are prepared from scratch using produce from the shop and the farm, then served in a 'farmhouse kitchen' style, unfussy and homely, promoting our 'farm to fork' philosophy.

Over the past 12 years the shop has established itself in the area as a valued alternative to the numerous supermarkets, remaining popular amongst local food enthusiasts, catering for everyone from individuals to families to other businesses.

We are fortunate to have an amazing, highly motivated team of staff at Woodview, in the shop, café and on the farm, who share our values and without whom we could not have achieved the success we have. Together, we are looking at how we can take Woodview forward in the future.

MOROCCAN ROASTED LAMB SHANK

This lovely winter weekend warmer makes a tasty change from a Sunday roast. It's delicious served with couscous or creamed potatoes. For more authenticity, use a Moroccan argan oil instead of olive oil. – Chef Anita

1 tsp cayenne pepper

1 tsp paprika

1 tsp smoked paprika

2 tsp ground black pepper

1 tbsp turmeric

2 cinnamon sticks

4 Woodview Farm lamb shanks

2 tbsp olive oil or Moroccan argan oil

2cm root ginger, grated

2 large onions, peeled and grated

4 cloves of garlic, peeled and crushed

500ml lamb stock

1 jar of passata

800g tinned chopped tomatoes

50g dates, chopped

100g dried apricots

50g sultanas

75g flaked almonds

1 tbsp clear honey

Place all the dry spices in a bowl and mix. Rub the lamb shanks with half of the spice mix, putting the other half to one side for later. Preheat the oven to 160°c.

Heat the oil in a large ovenproof pot or tagine, then add the ginger, onion and garlic to soften over a low heat. Add the remaining spice mix and cook for 5 minutes, then transfer the contents of the pot to a bowl and set aside.

Using the same pot, brown the lamb shanks on all sides. When they have seared, put the onion, ginger and garlic mixture back in along with all the remaining ingredients. Keep back some of the almond flakes to sprinkle on top of the tagine before serving.

Place the pot in the oven and cook for approximately 3 hours or until everything is tender. Serve on the bone with creamy mash and seasonal vegetables or Moroccan couscous.

PREPARATION TIME: 30 MINUTES | COOKING TIME: 3 HOURS 15 MINUTES | SERVES: 4

DIRECTORY

· ·

The Bear and Blacksmith
Chillington
South Devon
TQ7 2LD
Telephone: 01548 581171
Email: thebearandblacksmith@gmail.com
Website: thebearandblacksmith.com
An ultra-local pub for visitors and locals alike, responsibly sourcing our produce from our own farm and local suppliers.

Beeswax Dyson Farming
The Estate Office
Cyclone Way
Nocton
Lincolnshire
LN4 2GR
Telephone: 01526 322058
Email: enquiries@beeswaxdyson.com
Website: www.beeswaxdyson.com
Social Media: @beeswaxfarming
Innovative farming for the future in Lincolnshire, Oxfordshire and Gloucestershire.

Bigton House
Bigton
Shetland
ZE2 9JA
Telephone: 01950422397
Facebook: Bigton Farm
Twitter: @bigtonfarm
Instagram: @bigtonfarm
Mixed farm in Shetland rearing beef and sheep as well as growing small quantities of barley.

The Black Farmer
B109 Parkhall Business Centre
40 Martell Road
London
SE21 8EN
Telephone: 020 3735 6539
Website: www.theblackfarmer.com
Email: wilfred@theblackfarmer.com
Social Media: @theblackfarmer
The Black Farmer is a champion of British farming, producing great tasting, good quality, gluten-free food.

Black Swan Oldstead
Oldstead
York
YO61 4BL
Email: reception@blackswanoldstead.co.uk
Website: www.blackswanoldstead.co.uk
Instagram: @blackswan_oldstead
Facebook: BlackSwanOldstead
Michelin-starred restaurant with rooms on the edge of the North York Moors, with a three acre kitchen garden providing fresh produce daily. Run by the Banks family who have farmed the land at Oldstead for generations.

Brothers Farm Ltd
(Trading as Trehane Blueberry PYO)
Trehane Nursery
Stapehill Road
Wimborne
Dorset
BH21 7ND
Head Farmer Josh Benson: 07788 267031
Websites: www.trehaneblueberrypyo.co.uk
www.brothersfarm.co.uk
Instagram: @brothersfarmdorset
Facebook: bensonandbenson.bros
Organic blueberry farm in East Dorset. Wholesale and Pick Your Own with cut flowers and seasonal café.

Broughgammon Farm
50 Straid Road
Ballycastle
BT546NP
Telephone: 07976270465
Website: www.broughgammon.com
Facebook: Broughgammon Farm
Instagram: @broughgammonfrm
Forward-thinking, sustainable farm with regular events, supper clubs and a growing online meat box service. We rear cabrito kid goat meat, free-range rose veal and seasonal wild game, and produce vegetables for our shop.

Burwash Manor Farm
New Road
Barton
Cambridge
CB23 7EY
Telephone: 07774 186486
Website: www.burwashmanor.com
400 acre, mixed arable and livestock organic working farm. We also have an HLS scheme in place, are using the best methods of conservation possible, and sell home-grown produce in our on-site farm shop, The Larder.

Caldecote Manor Farm
Abbotsley Farms Ltd
Abbotlsey
St Neots
Cambridgeshire
PE19 6XQ
Telephone: 01480 880600
Instagram: @caldecotemanor / @caldecotemanorshoot
Diverse agricultural business with an emphasis on conservation, biodiversity, game management and diversification.

Caldecott Turkey Farms Limited
Holly Farm
Batemans Lane
Wythall
Worcestershire
B47 6NG
Telephone: 01564829380
Email: rob@caldecotts.co.uk and anne@caldecotts.co.uk
Website: www.caldecotts.co.uk
Ethical, passionate and committed farmers producing high welfare, free-range turkey and chicken.

Castle Farm
Redmans Lane
Shoreham
Sevenoaks
Kent
TN14 7UB
Telephone: 01959 523219
Website: www.castlefarmkent.co.uk
Social Media: @CastleFarmKent
Award-winning family farm and the UK's largest lavender farm. Our lovely farm shop is open daily, and you can also shop online.

South Devon Chilli Farm
Wigford Cross
Loddiswell
Kingsbridge TQ7 4DX
Telephone: 01548 550782
Website: www.sdcf.co.uk / www.southdevonchillifarm.co.uk
Social Media: @SDCF or @southdevonchillifarm
UK chilli grower and producer of chilli preserves, sauces and chilli chocolates. On-site farm shop and café, open all year.

Daylesford
Daylesford Farmshop
Daylesford, near Kingham
Gloucestershire
GL56 0YG
Telephone: 01608 731700
Social Media: @daylesfordfarm
At Daylesford we have been farming organically for over 40 years with a simple passion for real food. Visit our organic farm shops and cafés in the Cotswolds and London.

Eastbrook Farm
Bishopstone
SN6 8PP
Website: www.helenbrowningorganics.co.uk
Mixed organic farm, dining pub with great rooms, farm safaris, photography hides. For details, and where to buy see our website and read our book, PIG: Tales from an Organic Farm.

English Farm
Nuffield
Henley-on-Thames
Oxfordshire
RG9 5TH
Telephone: 01491 641 125
Website: englishfarm.net
Instagram: @englishfarm_
Producers of organic pasture-fed Longhorn beef. Working with nature to enhance the environment, biodiversity, animal welfare and produce outstanding food.

Essington Farm
Bognop Road
Essington
Wolverhampton
WV11 2AZ
Telephone: 01902 735 724
Email: info@essingtonfarm.co.uk
Website: www.essingtonfarm.co.uk
Facebook, Twitter and Instagram: @Essington Farm
Essington Farm has an award-winning farm shop, tearoom and Pick Your Own. It has farmed and retailed quality produce since 1892.

Fir Farm Ltd
Rectory Farm
Lower Swell
Gloucestershire
GL54 1LH
Telephone: 01451 828144
Website: www.firfarm.co.uk
Fir Farm is a 700 acre mixed livestock farm raising native and rare breed animals using sustainable, high welfare practices, working towards creating a fully sustainable, closed-loop farming system.

Fuller's Hill Farm
Cambridgeshire
SG19 3BP
Telephone (for bookings): 07544 208959
Email (for bookings): bookings@fullershillcottages.co.uk
Websites: www.fullershillcottages.co.uk / www. fullershillretreat.co.uk / www.fullershillweddings.co.uk
Facebook: Fullers Hill Cottages Official
Twitter: @fullershill and @jethro777777
Instagram: @fullershill.cottages
Fuller's Hill Farm is family-run and includes self-catering cottages, retreats and weddings. We also have a small airfield and aviation related business.

O. Jones and Sons
Bwthyn Tyn Llwyfan
Lon Niwri
Llanfairfechan
Conwy
LL33 0EU
Email: tynllwyfan@aol.com
Twitter: @1GarethWynJones
Facebook: GarethWynJones
Gareth is known as the 'Tweeting Farmer'. He serves to bridge the gap between town and country and campaigns for the production of sustainable, seasonal, local food.

The Garlic Farm
Mersley Lane
Newchurch
Isle of Wight
PO36 0NR
Telephone: 01983 865378
Website: www.thegarlicfarm.co.uk
Third-generation family business focused on excellent quality garlic production and sourcing, as well as the creation of over 60 products using garlic.

Graig Farm Organics

Tyn Y Fron
Mochdre
Newtown
Powys
SY16 4JW
Telephone: 01686 627979
Email: sales@graigfarm.co.uk
Website: www.graigfarm.co.uk
At Graig Farm I aim to keep things as traditional as possible and I look to the past in order to create a better future.

Greens of Devon and Silverton Wine

Silverton Vineyard
Devon
Websites: www.greensofdevon.com / www.silvertonwine.co.uk
Facebook: Greens of Devon and Silverton Vineyard
Instagram: @greensofdevon and @silvertonvineyard
Vineyard and edible flower and herb growers, working sustainably with nature to create beautiful food and drink.

W. F. Heady & Sons

Ash Farm
Drayton Parlsow
Milton Keynes
Contact: Richard Heady
Email: headyherd@hotmail.com
Instagram, Twitter & Facebook: @headysfarm
A mixed family farm producing grass-fed beef and lamb, wheat, barley, oats and oilseed rape in a sensitive and sustainable way.

Hirst Farms Ltd

Carr Farm
Ormesby
Great Yarmouth
Norfolk
NR29 3LG
Email: richard@hirstfarms.co.uk
Website: hirstysfamilyfunpark.co.uk
East Norfolk mixed farming business with arable cropping, sheep, cattle and pigs. We also have a 50 horse livery yard and seasonal farm park, Hirsty's Family Funpark.

The Home Farmer

Thorngarth Home Farm
Thoralby Road
Aysgarth
North Yorkshire
DL8 3AG
Telephone: 07808792261
Website: www.thehomefarmer.co.uk
Social Media (Facebook, Instagram & Twitter): @thehomefarmer
Dairy farm in Wensleydale, Yorkshire Dales. We make farmhouse Wensleydale cheese and sell fresh milk from our mobile milk vending machine.

JW & PA Stanley & Son

Spring Barrow Lodge
Swannymote Road
Coalville
Leicestershire
LE67 5UT
Telephone: 01509 503276
Website: www.blackbrooklonghorns.co.uk
Twitter: @JoeWStanley or @BlackbrookLong1
We are a small family beef and arable farm with a diversified farmyard animal art gallery.

La Hogue Farm Shop and Café

Chippenham
Newmarket
CB7 5PZ
Telephone: 01638 751128
Website: www.lahogue.co.uk
Facebook: La Hogue Farm
Award-winning farm shop and large café/restaurant situated just off the A11 near Newmarket, with a Certificate of Excellence from Trip Advisor.

Lowe & Co
School Farm
Hassall
Sandbach
Cheshire
CW11 4SA
Telephone: 07872664582
Instagram: @thefemalefarmer
Organic dairy farm producing milk for Belton Farm.

Moss Valley Fine Meats
Povey Farm
Lightwood Lane
Sheffield
S8 8BG
Telephone: 0114 2399922 / 07976434206
Email: srt@mossvalleyfinemeats.co.uk
Website: www.mossvalleyfinemeats.co.uk
*We produce pork, bacon, ham and sausages in our own butchery
from pigs bred and reared on our farm in the beautiful Moss
Valley close to the Sheffield-Derbyshire border.*

Pearson Gape Farming Partnership
Email: manorfarmcaxton@gmail.com
*PGFP is a regenerative agriculture arable family farming business
with an emphasis on net-zero carbon and positive community
impact.*

P.X. Farms Ltd
Estate Office
Scotland Farm
Scotland Road
Dry Drayton
Cambridge
CB23 8BN
Telephone: 01954 210211
Email: farmadmin@pxfarms.com
YouTube: https://www.youtube.com/pxfarmsltd
Twitter: @Pxfarms and @PXFarmsHaulage
*P.X. Farms is a family agribusiness for modern agriculture,
embracing diversification.*

Rooted in Hull Ltd.
Website: www.rootedinhull.org.uk
Twitter: @rootedinhull
Facebook: @RootedinHull
Instagram: @fishrooted
LinkedIn: Adrian Fisher
*Creating a space in the heart of the city for growing fruit and
vegetables, sharing knowledge of livestock, fish and meat, and
providing a venue where all of this can be celebrated.*

Saxby's Cider
The Cideryard
Grange Farm
Farndish
Wellingborough
Northants
NN29 7HJ
Telephone: 01933 353666
Website: www.saxbyscider.co.uk
*Makers of craft ciders and general experimenters in new and
wonderful concoctions.*

Sharpham Cheese Dairy
Sharpham Estate
Ashprington
Totnes
Devon
TQ9 7UT
Telephone: 01803 732600
Email: info@sharphamcheese.co.uk
Social Media: @sharphamcheese
*Home of our famous Brie, Rustic and Ticklemore cheeses,
handcrafted with milk from our own herd of Jersey cows, along
with goat's and ewe's milk from our West Country neighbours.*

South Farm

Shingay-cum-Wendy
Royston
Cambridgeshire
SG8 0HR
Telephone: 01223 207581
Website: www.south-farm.co.uk
Email: info@south-farm.co.uk
Social Media: @southfarm1
Pinterest: www.pinterest.co.uk/chwv/south-farm-weddings
This vibrant working farm provides the perfect backdrop for beautiful weddings in the stunning Cambridgeshire countryside. The productive smallholding uses organic principles to supply a rich variety of seasonal produce, catering in-house for delicious wedding breakfasts.

South Farm

Budleigh Salterton
Devon
EX9 7AY
Contact: Jemma Pyne
Telephone: 07968820541
Instagram and Facebook: @pynesfarmshop
Beautiful farm on the south west coast of Devon producing wheat, barley, maize and a variety of vegetables alongside a small flock of sheep for lamb, and 600 free-range chickens for eggs.

Tractors and Tweed

Website: www.tractorsandtweed.com
Instagram: @TractorsandTweed
To follow my journey of juggling farming, family and work please follow me on my Instagram account, blog and YouTube channel.

Little Lowlands

Lowlands Farm
Illey Lane
Halesowen
B62 0HJ
Website: www.littlelowlands.co.uk
If you fancy a farming experience that will make memories like no other, then take a look at our courses online.

The Wife Behind The Farmer

Instagram: @hannah_l_morgan
Twitter: @hannah_l_morgan
Facebook: The Wife Behind The Farmer.
Email: thewifebehindthefarmer@outlook.com
Website: www.thewifebehindthefarmer.co.uk
Blog and social media accounts covering all things country, specialising in supporting other women like me, Hannah Morgan, who have a role on the farm, yet want to pursue their own business too.

Will Evans

Telephone: 07841 747 934
Email: will@rockandrollfarming.com / will@eatfarmnow.com
Website: www.rockandrollfarming.com / www.eatfarmnow.com
Social Media: @willpenrievans @RandRFarmingPod @eatfarmnow
As well as being a full time farmer, Will is the producer and host of the award-winning Rock & Roll Farming Podcast, and co-founder and community manager of Eat Farm Now.

Woodview Farm Shop

Mill Hill
Potton Road
Gamlingay
SG19 3LW
Telephone: 01767 650200 (shop) and 01767 651667 (café)
Website: www.woodviewfarm.co.uk
Email: info@woodviewfarm.co.uk
Facebook: woodviewfarmshop
Independent, local, family-run farm shop and café promoting farm to fork values.